T0152675

SAVE YOUR ASKS

PRAISE FOR *SAVE YOUR ASKS*

Many authors, including myself for *The Millennial Whisperer*, waste their asks with very influential people asking for endorsements of their book.

What is most important to me is that this content connects with you. What I care about more is what you think, not them.

So, for this book, I decided to save my asks and let the content speak for itself.

SAVE YOUR ASKS

Evolve Your Networking Currencies.
Grow Your Influence. Triple Your Business.

CHRIS TUFF

PANTA PRESS

NEW YORK

LONDON • NASHVILLE • MELBOURNE • VANCOUVER

SAVE YOUR ASKS

Evolve Your Networking Currencies, Grow Your Influence.
Triple Your Business

Published in New York, New York, by Morgan James Publishing in partnership with Panta Press. Morgan James is a trademark of Morgan James, LLC. www.MorganJamesPublishing.com

Proudly distributed by Ingram Publisher Services.

Morgan James BOGO™

A **FREE** ebook edition is available for you or a friend with the purchase of this print book.

_____

CLEARLY SIGN YOUR NAME ABOVE

Instructions to claim your free ebook edition:
1. Visit MorganJamesBOGO.com
2. Sign your name CLEARLY in the space above
3. Complete the form and submit a photo of this entire page
4. You or your friend can download the ebook to your preferred device

ISBN 9781631956270 paperback
ISBN 9781631956287 ebook
ISBN 9781631956294 hardcover
Library of Congress Control Number:
2021938195

Cover Design by:
John Stapleton

Interior Design by:
Chris Treccani
www.3dogcreative.net

Morgan James is a proud partner of Habitat for Humanity Peninsula and Greater Williamsburg. Partners in building since 2006.

Get involved today! Visit MorganJamesPublishing.com/giving-back

CONTENTS

DEDICATION

To my amazingly supportive wife, Julie, who always believes in my dreams and who doesn't get too annoyed as I try to inspire and connect in every waking moment of every day.

To my two daughters, Finley and Marlin, I hope you can continue to hone your tenacity and resilience, and I hope this book will allow you both to "ruthlessly pursue your passions."

FOREWORD

In April 2019, I published *The Most Powerful Woman in the Room Is You*, a book to inspire and motivate women to find confidence in their voice and learn how to sell their way to success.

As the lead charity auctioneer for Christie's auction house based in New York City, I had spent more than 16 years onstage raising money for nonprofits around the world. As I stood backstage before hundreds of auctions, waiting as we neared the moment when I would stride purposefully onstage, hammer down the gavel, and start the auction, there was inevitably someone who wasn't a seasoned performer who would begin to list all of the things they couldn't do: (1) they could never ask anyone for money, (2) they could never get onstage and ask anyone for anything, or (3) they just didn't have the confidence to ask. Period.

This realization, coupled with the fact that I was nearing my second decade working at Christie's, made me feel like it was time for a new challenge, a new adventure, something to push me outside of my comfort zone. I decided to write a book that would address these issues and help other people gain the confidence that I had after so many years onstage.

After a year of writing and editing *The Most Powerful Woman in the Room Is You*, I published it and spent the next year touring the book around the world. While I originally thought that the greatest gift of writing a book would be simply getting to say that I actually wrote a book, I realized that the greatest gift was that it allowed me the opportunity to meet so many amazing people outside of my immediate circle.

Every city I visited on a book talk, every speech I gave for a group of people, expanded my network and gave me access to new ideas and, more importantly, a new point of view. So many new relationships were formed and built by simply putting myself out there and interacting with people all over the world.

When the global pandemic brought New York City and the rest of the country to a grinding halt, we were in Colorado on a spring break trip with our kids. As we watched from afar as the news from our city became increasingly frightening, we decided to stay in Colorado until it felt safe to return.

As a family that is used to living in the bustling, busy, wall-to-wall people of New York City, the contrast of living in total isolation in the mountains of Colorado was stark. Beautiful as it was to watch the snow falling on the mountains, as a woman who grew up in southern Louisiana, I woke up every day hoping that the snow would stop. Moreover, as someone who was used to being on stage weekly for charity auctions and speaking engagements, I felt like a huge part of my existence had been completely stripped away. Like most people, I felt alone and desperately craved the connectivity that had been such a huge part of my life only months before. In addition, most of the charities I worked with hadn't been able to hold their fundraising galas because of the pandemic. One in particular reached out to tell me that their food bank was circling the city block four times. They needed help.

I did the only thing I could think of doing at that moment.

I asked.

I asked entrepreneurs, celebrities, people I had known my entire life, others I had never met. I asked them to join me on IG Live and give advice about business, life, and mental health. Anything I could think of to help anyone out there who needed a boost of inspiration to keep going during such a dark period. The only thing I asked was that every person who joined me would donate to The River Fund in exchange for the advice. I had saved my ask and the result was an inbox flooded with people who wanted to introduce me to their connections who were looking to help people realize their potential.

In that flooded inbox was an email from a close friend asking if she could introduce me to a college friend, Chris Tuff. She had tuned into my IG Live every day to watch and decided that I should meet another person who felt compelled to turn on the light for other people in this darkest period of our lives.

Chris and I emailed back and forth before deciding to hop on Zoom for an hour. He was in the process of writing a book and wanted to connect. We spent an hour talking about his concept for this book.

I was immediately drawn to Chris. His confidence is evident from the minute you meet him, but it is his warmth that draws you in. There is no question that he understands confidence is the key to life, but he doesn't want to shield that information from anyone seeking more from their own life. Rather he wants to share that information with the world. In this book, Chris has created the handbook for everyone looking to pursue their passion by building great relationships.

Save Your Asks not only shares a proven method for identifying and pursuing passion but also walks you through the steps it takes to naturally build strong connections. As I learned during the pandemic, when everything else has fallen apart, those relationships will keep you afloat, deepen your life, and allow you to gain a deeper knowledge and understanding of the world around you.

Chris will help anyone looking to pursue their passion by building strong, lasting relationships. He will show you how speaking with your authentic self will help you forge the path for the life you want to lead. He will teach you to live with a positive outlook and show you the importance of a strong mindset.

And, most importantly, he will teach you to Save Your Asks.

—Lydia Fenet

PREFACE

In 2018, I took time away from the advertising agency of which I am a partner to write and release my first book, *The Millennial Whisperer*, about how to lead millennials well in the workplace. That book became a runaway success—more so than I could have ever imagined. We were getting a lot of traction at the beginning of 2020—right when the COVID-19 pandemic was really hitting the U.S.

I was scheduled to be speaking at Nike, sharing the big stage with its new president, Heidi O'Neill, in front of all its sales teams. It was a big engagement, and I was extremely excited (for those who know me, this is not an uncommon emotion).

Then I got the call, as the world shut down, that the gig was no longer going to happen. Though none of us could have predicted the pandemic outcome, I knew Nike was not going to be able to reschedule the event anytime soon.

My heart sunk. It had been my dream for quite some time to impact people in a positive way beyond what I had been able to do at my advertising agency, and this Nike engagement was one of my biggest opportunities to do so. I had been so excited to present in front of so many people at Nike, knowing that the positive impact I could make on those people would continue to grow as each of them impacted others. And now it was canceled. I was dizzy with disappointment. What would I do now?

Then something hit me. Just two years earlier, I had been relatively unknown outside of the advertising world. But then I wrote and published a book that would land on multiple national bestseller lists and helped thousands upon thousands of people. Taking that leap to writing a book about a subject so close to my heart is what gave me the opportunity to be booked alongside the new CEO of one of the most prolific brands in the world—an honor I would never have imagined before writing *The Millennial Whisperer*. Sure, it was canceled, but the fact that it was scheduled in the first place was a dream come true.

I wondered: How could someone like me, who was relatively well known in the advertising world but completely unknown in the leadership development world get booked for such a high-profile opportunity in less than two years?

And then it hit me: connection.

When I wrote *The Millennial Whisperer*, my goal was to help younger and older generations work well together in a productive, collaborative, fulfilling, and impactful way. I was so passionate about this goal that I naturally connected with leaders from around the world to help them create better workplaces for themselves and their team members. I showed up to every call, meeting, or event with the ultimate goal of making an impact. By doing so, I quickly built trust and authentic connections with executives at companies all around the world. Those connections enabled me to get hired for speeches, consulting projects, and coaching opportunities at notable companies. And those companies were confident in hiring me because I demonstrated to them an authentic desire to help. I had built real connections with them on a human level.

I then started thinking about my experiences working with these organizations. Whenever I'd go in, I'd make a point to learn the pain points of organizations, companies, and individuals before making any suggestions about improvements they could make. And, although every company's struggles are unique, the companies that struggled with building relationships with employees or customers shared one common gap: a loss of genuine connection with each other and with their customers.

So there I was, sulking a bit but reflecting a lot, and I was reminded about some advice I had received a long time ago about success: success doesn't come from never facing challenges; it comes from being resilient in the face of challenges. I then remembered a rule I have. I call it my *two-hour rule*: when something doesn't go my way, I can dwell on it for two hours, but then I have to come up with a plan to bounce back.

It had only been 20 minutes, but I could feel myself shifting into a new perspective already. And, unlike two years earlier, I had already built deep connections with people who were looking to improve their workplaces. I knew I could do the same thing for building meaningful connections in the workplace that I did through *The Millennial Whisperer* on the subject of intergenerational leadership. I could help a lot of people and increase my impact on the world.

Even better, as passionate as I am about intergenerational leadership, *nothing* compares to my passion for and ability to make connections. Whether it be making mutually beneficial connections of people or discovering common points of connections between seemingly disconnected subject matter, my ability is second to none. This ability goes way back too. For example, when I was studying in London, I was enrolled in five very different classes, including The History of London and Modern Art and Architecture in England. At the end of the semester, each class required a term paper. As I thought about what to write, I uncovered a common thread that allowed me to write and turn in the same term paper for all five classes. This was an innate skill I had before I really knew the value of it. Today, I've simply applied this ability to connecting people. And in the networking space, this means I am constantly the broker of what I call people's *currencies*: *What does one person need that another person in my network can provide?*

The more I thought about it, the more excited I became. And at that point, nothing was going to stop me from helping people and organizations build better and deeper connections. The book you're holding in your hands right now is the result of that commitment.

And I can guarantee you one thing.

You need this book. The world is moving faster than ever before, and the connection deficit is also much greater than ever!

But this book is not designed to make your life incrementally better. It's designed to help you completely transform your life. Take me, for example. In 2018, I was working in my agency relentlessly. I did great work and worked with incredible people, but my impact on the world was limited to the work I did for the agency.

Today I spend the majority of my days meeting with some of the most inspiring and interesting people in the world (some who are well known, and others who have yet to be discovered). In each of these meetings, I'm trying to dig into their currencies, unlock their dreams, and become a catalyst for making their missions happen. This might be helping an entrepreneur raise money for a lingerie start-up (please check out Giapenta) or coaching an executive at a Fortune 100 company to unlock her side hustle. Very little of my time is spent talking about advertising.

But guess what? My business development for my agency has never been more effective. In fact, I get more leads and meetings for my agency now than ever before. And it's all thanks to spending even more of my time doing what you'll learn in this book.

Richard Ward, the CEO of Guided by Good (the parent company of 22squared, where I work), and my immediate boss, Erica Hoholick, *know* that in order to unlock future new business, they must trust the process involved with me building these connections. They know that better and deeper relationships form when you aren't trying to "sell, sell, sell" and, instead, focus on building genuine connections with great people. They've seen it develop since I published *The Millennial Whisperer*. Now, they give me the freedom to truly run without having to see an immediate return on investment at 22squared (thank you, Richard and Erica!).

The same can be true for you too. The strategies I've included in this book can help you build more powerful and deeper connections that will also give you a new dose of fulfillment. You will learn how to

1. Look at networking in a new, much more energizing light
2. Discover your "currency" and the "passions" that empower new ambitions
3. Add new dimensions to your career, life, and relationships through these passions
4. Build a new network of genuine, lifelong connections
5. Triple your sales ability in business
6. And much more

Walking the Talk

To write this book, I could not just sit behind a computer and type away until everything I knew was organized on the page. After all, I had built my network and achieved success through connecting with others. So I needed to write the book that way as well. Sure, I'd include my strategies for networking and building connections, but I would also include stories and lessons from some of the most successful networkers in the world, many of whom suddenly had some downtime like I did.

And that's what I did. The results of my work, as you'll see, are pretty amazing. I get goosebumps just writing about it because, for the first time in my life, I can say this book, this movement, is why I was put on this earth. And it is my goal not to make a bunch of money with this thing, not to become famous, but to impact *at least one million lives. A million people whom I can help become better sellers and connectors while also allowing them to do this with greater purpose and fulfillment.* I can't wait for *you* to be one of them.

I *guarantee* you that with just a few small tweaks you will learn in this book, you'll find yourself both more successful at your job and enjoying life a heck of a lot more!

THE NEW NETWORKING TERMINOLOGY

Throughout this book, you'll come across these terms—a lot. So here's a brief primer.

Currency

This is a medium of exchange and how you monetize your value. Your currency (whether you care to admit it or not) is your expertise and what you get paid to do. If you're the person at Frito-Lay who stocks Publix shelves with chips, your currency is tidiness, organization, and esoteric knowledge about grocery store products. If you're a DJ, your currency is mixing music. If you're a dentist, your currency is dental hygiene and teeth. Your currency can translate over to new careers and new opportunities for connection (but as you'll learn, you need to be responsible and patient here).

Super-Connectors

These are the people who seem to know someone for anything you need. These are the people whose currency is actually making *connections*.

Askholes

I always try to be positive and constructive, but not everybody is wired this way. You know those people in your life who go in for three asks in a row without even saying "Thanks"? Those are askholes. They are takers. They are selfish (they often don't *know* any better so feel free to send them this book as a gift). They might be good people overall, but they are way too internally focused on their networking and relationship building.

If you're an askhole, people don't want to make connections for you because they don't want their connections to be annoyed. If they do, they're likely to make halfhearted connections. And they're not going to connect you with their best contacts. Don't be an askhole.

Empty Askers

Empty askers are people who try to dress up an ask as something different. They might ask to tag along with you and a highly successful contact of yours as a guise to "continue our conversation" when they really just want to build a relationship with your contact. Or they might ask if they can join you on a run because they know you also run with someone they want to meet. Or they ask to go out to a game sometime knowing that you have season tickets and will likely offer to use your tickets instead of having them buy tickets.

With all these examples, the "ask" was empty in that it was disguised as a genuine attempt to connect. Sometimes, people make an empty ask in order to create a connection or be immediately "liked" with no real intention of delivering on that promise. For example: "I'd love to have you for dinner when you're in town!" But when that time comes, you really *do not* want to have them over for dinner. (I'll share a common example from my life later in the book too.)

Shawshanking

This is the art of developing relationships over time. Chip away every day, just like Andy Dufresne in *The Shawshank Redemption* when he mails a letter a week asking for funds for the prison library.

Relationships are created over time and with light touchpoints. Commenting on a prospect's Instagram account, texting, emailing, calling—these are all paths toward the verb *shawshanking*. Patience and persistence are far more valuable in the new world of easy access to almost anyone. The key here is slowly deepening that relationship and connection every time.

Race to the Middle

How fast can you find a middle, common passion point between you and the person you are meeting or talking to? This could be a sports team, a hobby, a movie, or a place they live that you've visited. This is the catalyst of what takes small talk to the next level. This is you taking a vested interest in something they're also passionate about and connecting around it genuinely—this is *authentic* connection.

We'll talk later about the importance of *curiosity* in creating and deepening relationships in networking, but it's one of the greatest missing pieces out there today. When you're racing to the middle to find a common ground, you're curiously digging into their lives, passions, and interests.

Because the race to the middle is something people traditionally struggle with, let me add a word of encouragement and an example to this definition.

First, a word of encouragement: Your race to the middle doesn't have to be some awkward moment where you both ask each other what you like ("Do you like cars? How about sports? Art?"). The easiest way to find your "middle" is to ask people about themselves and listen. When you meet people, you will generally know at least one thing that you have in common, such as a common friend or that you both have kids. Ask them about that commonality, such as "How do you know Chris?" or "Your daughter Angela really works hard in softball. She get that from you?" Then listen. Listen for hints, such as "I met Chris at a networking event." Ask about the networking event, what they are looking to build by networking, etc. Keep asking about them. Almost without fail, if you're in the same room as someone, you *will* have a common interest that you can find if you ask enough questions.

Here's an example of how this could work. In 2019, I was on a kiteboarding trip with two of my best friends, Pete Boulden and Hank McLarty. When I found my seat on the plane, I noticed Pete talking to a couple I recognized from TV (and their related massive cult following): Kim Zolciak and Kroy Biermann. I sat down, said hello, and just listened. They talked with Pete about their show and some of their business goals.

During that conversation, the idea of Kim writing a book came up. Having just written *The Millennial Whisperer*, I was able to share advice and even offered to connect them with my book strategist. Boom! Race to the middle. By the time we landed, the whole cabin must have had their noise-canceling headphones cranking because of how loud and enthusiastic Kim and I were. We've since become genuine friends, and Kim and Kroy will use me as a sounding board for their business endeavors. Once again doing business with people is a byproduct of genuine connection!

INTRODUCTION

Surfer Raimana Van Bastolaer has spent most of his life disconnecting from everything most people chase. And yet, he's one of the most connected people I know; a nonstop networker who brings pure joy to everyone he meets. He's also one of the greatest super-connectors in the world. You may ask yourself, how does a surfer who spends most of his time in the middle of French Polynesia become one of the most connected people on the planet? Well, he lives his life where his passions, talents, and "networking currency" (surfing) collide. That attracts people to him and makes building his connections a natural outcome of the way he lives his life.

Raimana is legendary at Kelly Slater's Surf Ranch (home to the most exclusive man-made wave in the world) and Teahupo'o (the gnarliest wave in the world). Raimana knows the waves of Teahupo'o better than almost anybody else on this planet. To watch him ride a wave is to watch a force of nature, and to talk with him is to talk with a man who embraces his power to connect with other people. This ability to connect has allowed him to pursue his passion while making a massive impact on his community.

"Raimana is also one of the sport's greatest ambassadors," writes Jamie Brisick for Outerknown.[1] "He has shared his native Tahiti with thousands of traveling wave riders. World Surf League commentator Strider Wasilewski knows all about this. He and Raimana have been close friends for many years. 'Very few people open their home and heart to surfers traveling through where they live the way Raimana does,' said Strider over email. 'He'll help people out without even knowing them. A guy's boat burned down—Raimana found out and gave him money to get home, and didn't even ask for it back. Raimana is connected to people everywhere, a pure connection of aloha and good mana. No matter the color, no matter the finance, billionaires to bums—Raimana is connected!'"

I was introduced to Raimana by a guy named Jasen Trautwein, who you'll meet later in the book. When I asked Jasen at the end of one of our meetings, "Who's the one person in your ridiculous network of super-connectors I have to meet?" he told me I *had* to meet Raimana. Knowing the surfing world very well, I asked, "The Raimana who's partnered with Kelly Slater, the one who almost lost his head by a Jet Ski at Teahupo'o?!" Yep, that Raimana.

Jasen then shared the story of when he first met Raimana on the back of a Jet Ski. For those of you not familiar with big-wave surfing, the only way to access the waves is for someone to tow you and your surfboard to catch the waves. You can't just paddle yourself out there like you can surfing small waves off the beach. Raimana was towing Jasen on the back of his Jet Ski. Most of the time, the person towing you wishes you good luck and turns back to shore. Not Raimana. Raimana knows every person he encounters shares at least one passion with him—a passion for big-wave

---

1   James Brisick, "The Voice of Hope: Surfing with Raimana," *Outerknown* (blog), accessed June 23, 2021, https://www.outerknown.com/blogs/journey/the-voice-of-hope-surfing-with-raimana.

surfing—and likely many others. So when he tows people out, he takes that as an opportunity to make a deeper connection.

"I love you, bruddah," said Raimana as he pushed Jasen off the Jet Ski. And just like that, they were bonded for life.

You see, it is *genuine connection* that makes relationships last a lifetime.

And sometimes the universe has a way of giving you the signs that you're on the right track, that you're doing the right thing. Two weeks after I interviewed Raimana on FaceTime, I was kiteboarding the Outer Banks with two of my best friends, Hank McLarty and Pete Boulden, for my 40th birthday. After kiting more than 70 miles, we were sitting at a picnic table, talking about the epicness of the day over fish tacos and Topo Chicos.

I heard a familiar voice through somebody's smartphone. It was Raimana. I knew it. I could never forget that voice and the passion with which he spoke. Never one to shy away from meeting someone new, I turned to the nearby table from where the sound was coming.

"Are you guys talking to Raimana?" I yelled. Sure enough, they were FaceTiming with Raimana, who was in the middle of French Polynesia. I popped in on the call, all of us amazed at how small the world can be. From the other side of the world, he had just connected me with a new network of kiteboarding friends from California.

Raimana Van Bastolaer is one of the 40-plus people I had the great fortune to interview for this book. His story of rising through the surfing world is a prime example of the art and science of saving your asks.

I asked Raimana why he pushes people away using the words, "I love you, bruddah." Is it deeper than knowing you met some-

4 | **SAVE YOUR ASKS**

one who shares a passion with you? Is it just a way of wishing good tidings? Or is it something more?

It turns out that it's all this and more. With those words, Raimana wants to send the message to the surfer that "This is your time. Appreciate it. Go for it right away. At the end of the wave, you can think about anything else. But enjoy the moment now." He is also saying, "This is a gnarly wave and you might die, so I want the last thing you hear from me to be *I love you.*" Raimana makes a bond for life in this moment because he is intentional about making a genuine connection.

Read This Before You Do Anything Else, Especially Starting a Side Hustle

Full Disclosure: I think *everyone* should have a side hustle, which we will discuss later.

But I also know that starting a side hustle, when done well, *improves* your performance in your primary job, contrary to popular opinion. For example, I have never been as productive at my agency than after I started my side hustle, writing *The Millennial Whisperer* and the book you hold in your hands. The key is to find the right side hustle and pursue it in a strategic way that causes your primary job to benefit as you build more momentum in your side hustle. When you do it this way, both your primary job and your side hustle become better because of each other.

If you run an organization, this might sound scary. But if you want better employee retention and happier and more fulfilled employees, you must accept this. Even better, you should *encourage* them to pursue side hustles (as long as they do not compete with your company and offerings, of course).

Moreover, getting team members into more of an entrepreneurial mindset will shift the way they look at their jobs. As my friend, Vincent Pugliese, who leads a mastermind community called Total Life Freedom, says, "We're not being taught to be entrepreneurial. We're taught to get on a bus, follow orders, stand in line, and not question authority. By 10 years old, this robs kids of so much of their curiosity and puts them on a path away from entrepreneurship."

Vincent has helped hundreds of people start and grow side hustles. In doing so, he is constantly amazed by how much each side hustle impacts employees, even if they never intend to turn those side hustles into full-time hustles. "A job is where dreams go to die," Vincent explains. "Jobs kill more dreams than anything else. People set their expenses based on their salary and end up with car payments, mortgages, and debt. They become dependent on the job. By their 20s, they often give up on any dream of starting their own business. When someone ends up in that situation, one of the only ways to escape without going into even more debt is to use a side hustle to lower expenses and increase income."

But again, starting a side hustle *doesn't* mean building something that takes you away from your main job. In many cases, just the opposite is true: people build side hustles that make them better at their main jobs. They use their side hustle to make connections that increase sales for their main job—just like *The Millennial Whisperer* led to me landing several new clients for my ad agency. And the same is true with this book. I've made many connections from writing this book that led directly to opportunities for my agency.

In other words, a side hustle might be just what you need to improve your results in your day job. Among other reasons, side hustles position you to build connections in your comfort zones. If you focus on using your side hustles to build relationships with people who could benefit from what you do at your primary job, your side hustle—whether you pursue it for profit or passion—will frequently lead to dramatically improved results at your day job.

"I always loved *Wind, Sand and Stars* by Antoine de Saint Exupéry. It's the greatest adventure book of all time. And it always paired with one of the things I wanted to do, which was to not have a boring life and do things that were different. It was very different from my college buddies, who just wanted to work in private equity from the time they were six years old." —Shane Emmett, cofounder of Health Warrior

If you've read *The Millennial Whisperer*, you know I believe companies can become destination employers where people go to *live* their dreams, and not where dreams go to die. Thus, I don't take as extreme a view about jobs as Vincent does. But the truth is that many companies don't do what it takes to help their employees become both productive and fulfilled. So the reality is that many jobs *are* where dreams go to die, even if they don't have to be.

That's where side hustles can come in. Side hustles can fuel your passion and give you extra income to break free from financial dependence on a single paycheck. They can give you the financial flexibility to take more control over your career—either by finding a job that's a better fit (in which case everyone wins by you leaving your job) or by turning your side hustle into your main hustle. Some side hustles can even help you develop skills to make lateral moves within your company to a position you enjoy and will be more effective in, even if it requires taking a temporary pay cut while you prove yourself again. (If your side hustle earns you some income, it gives you the financial flexibility to make a move to a better fit without worrying as much about if it comes with a pay cut. In the long run, everyone will win with you working in a position that uses your passions and talents.).

Along these lines, if you currently lead a team or run an organization, allow people to make lateral moves within your organization. Otherwise, you could lose your best team members. Remember, *The Millennial Whisperer* and this book were both side hustles for me, which my partners at 22squared and Guided by Good embrace, knowing that a byproduct will be more connections and business for the agency.

Using Currency to Build Connection

When I share the concept of using our currencies to build connections, some people turn to me and say, "Chris, I have no *real* expertise or connections high up in a company to barter with people and no real other currency to offer."

Some of these people are fresh out of college or relatively new to the workforce. Others are more experienced but don't see themselves as "experts" on any subject people value or don't see themselves as "well connected." The truth is, *everyone* has something to offer, and it doesn't need to be sophisticated, fancy, or expensive. Frankly, two of the highest value networking tools around are simply following up with people and helping them make connections. Following up with people is easy. You don't need any special skills or experience. You just need to take action. And connecting people doesn't require any special knowledge. It just takes a little effort. When you're starting out, you might need to ask around for useful connections to pass along. Over time, you will be able to make more and better connections yourself. But taking action will set you apart from the vast majority of people in the business world.

A friend of mine shared a rule he has with me when it comes to his networking currency of following up and being a connector: "If someone comes to mind, I text or email them and let them know. I keep it really simple by just writing, 'You came to mind today, so I figured I'd touch base and say hello. I hope you're doing well.' I can't tell you how many times the person has written back letting me know they had been thinking about me too and had an opportunity they wanted to talk about with me."

Take action. It doesn't have to be giving them a fancy gift; it could just be texting words of encouragement. You might not know where it will lead you but just trust the process. And, as I tell audiences, "The worst thing you could do is nothing at all."

Make the Connection

Each chapter in *Save Your Asks* ends with this call to action: Make the Connection.

In it, I'll share with you a simple list of proven tactics to help you navigate this new world of networking and start applying the strategies discussed in that chapter. Take action on those tactics and you'll start building momentum toward a better business, better life, or both.

So when you get to the end of each chapter, please don't treat them as a simple summary. Treat them as a to-do list. There may be things on these lists that you don't want to do—outsource them or do them *first*. Make the connection between this book and your life.

And I invite you to make the connection with me, too, by visiting my website (christuff.me) or emailing me at chris@christuff.me. No need to send me a bouquet of flowers. Shoot me an email or, if you want to get the best (and likely fastest) response, shawshank me on Instagram at @tuff22.

Buckle up and get fired up! It's time to take a new direction toward connection!

PART 1:

YOUR PLAN

CHAPTER 1:

The Problem with Networking

Going once, going twice … *not* sold!

Meet Lydia Fenet, an auctioneer with more experience than almost anyone in the business today. A senior vice president at Christie's auction house in New York City and the founder and director of its international strategic partnerships program, Lydia's most important tool *isn't* her gavel—it's her smile, sense of humor and humility, and genuine sense of connection with almost anybody.

So when Matt Damon became a junior auctioneer at one of her fundraisers and completely flubbed her name while on stage, Lydia kept her cool, gracefully corrected him, and thanked "Mike Diamond, a dentist from Long Island" for supporting the event. Her seamless, graceful response built a strong rapport between the two.

After having thousands of conversations with some of the most successful people in the world, Lydia became a master of conversation, making even the most awkward moments feel natural. By seeing eye to eye with anybody, making eye contact with everybody, and refusing to accept the concept of a "nobody," Lydia Fenet has mastered the art of making everyone around her feel comfortable. Being able to engage in comfortable conversations with everyone—from dignitaries to the ultrawealthy and even real dentists from Long Island—has become a currency she has used to make connections with anyone she comes across. And she has used that currency and a natural "save your asks" mentality to build deep relationships with some of the most impressive people in the world.

"Everybody puts on their boots the same way in the morning," she says, reciting one of her father's favorite phrases. "No one is higher than you; no one is lower than you. We're all living the same life."

"Status is a zero-sum game ... The problem is, to win at a status game, you have to put somebody else down. That's why you should avoid status games in your life—because they make you into an angry, combative person. You're always fighting to put other people down and elevate yourself and the people you like." —**Naval Ravikant**

Lydia's approach exposes the big problem with typical networking—people go into it as if some people have a magical way of putting on their boots. They "rank" people and change the way they treat people based on where they think the person stacks up compared to them on the ladder of success. The "Matt Damons"

of the world intimidate them and get them to act fake while they don't bother with the "Mike Diamonds" of the world.

Lydia knows this is the wrong approach. She knows that the name written on the "Hello My Name Is" sticker doesn't mean the person is any different from her at their core. So she puts down the Sharpies, doesn't let the name tag change who she is, and says yes to the new world of networking that you'll learn throughout this chapter and the rest of the book.

The Problems with Traditional Networking Events

After reviewing dozens of studies, author David Burkus discovered that, by design, most networking events are doomed from the start. Columbia Business School professors, for example, surveyed executives before an event, finding 95 percent of them expressing a desire to meet new people. But the average attendee spent half their time with the one-third of people they already knew. The most successful networker at the event? The bartender.

"Schmoozing at a mixer is far less likely to lead you to a powerful network than jumping into projects, teams, or activities that draw a diverse set of people together," writes David Burkus in an article for *Harvard Business Review*.[2] "The return on investment of time in these types of activities is far higher than just attending a social event (and that's before you factor in the health benefits of sports leagues or the societal benefit of working with a charity) … So skip the networking events. You have permission to never attend one again … as long as you're reallocating that time to the right kind of shared activity."

---

2 David Burkus, "Go Ahead, Skip That Networking Event," *Harvard Business Review*, May 14, 2018, https://hbr.org/2018/05/go-ahead-skip-that-networking-event.

Having better alternatives isn't the only problem with most networking events. They almost inevitably end up forcing conversations about people's résumés, John's divorce, and how "busy" people's lives are. You often spend two hours listening to people brag and complain. Half the conversations are awkward and unproductive. The other half are way-too-long discussions about absolutely nothing helpful for making a meaningful connection.

My friend Rick, for example, flew to Florida for a four-day convention on coding amid all the COVID-19 travel hassles. He was hoping to meet people who might help him grow his coding business. Instead, he found himself awkwardly meeting strangers who were much more interested in stockpiling free vendor swag than making meaningful connections.

Networking events are also incredibly time-consuming, which Burkus also points out. If we all had an extra five hours a day (or even five hours a week), it wouldn't be as big a deal. But every hour we spend eating stale bagels and drinking burnt coffee is an hour we can't spend with our families, working on our businesses, exploring a hobby, or even just sleeping. So they *are* time-consuming and put the focus on the *process* of networking rather than on building authentic connections. Speed dating, name tags, and "once around the room" sessions are certainly helpful to get information quickly and add business cards to your pile of people with whom you'll never follow up. But they're not very helpful for making true, mutually beneficial connections.

Even formal networking groups often connect people based on obligations, not value, requiring people to make regular introductions or be kicked out of the group. And, if you spend all your free time going to networking groups, you cut out a *huge* segment of the market from your potential contact list. Specifically, you only connect with others who attend networking events. What about all the awesome introverts who have no interest in networking events? And what about all the awesome people who are so connected and busy that they don't have time to attend networking events? Those people are some of my best connections and deepest relationships. And I met *none* of them at networking events.

I could go on and on about the problems with traditional networking events, but I'd rather focus on what to do instead, so let me leave you with just one more problem. Networking can actually make your life worse, and not just from wasting your time and feeding you terrible food. They can become a distraction, a crutch, and even make you a terrible and transactional networker. You can become so used to three-minute introductions and forced connections that all of your relationship building becomes rushed and transactional.

As my friend, Quincy Jones, a super-connector and founding partner of SageStone Partners says, "Networking is not my passion. If you tell me to go to a networking event, trust me, it's the last thing in the world I want to do. But being able to connect with people and create something better for the world is really fun." In other words, networking is about the connection to Quincy, and not forced connections either. Approach him with an opportunity to participate in the right "projects, teams, or activities that draw a diverse set of people together," as Burkus suggests, and he'll be all in. Invite him to a "networking event," and he'll have very little interest. So, do yourself a favor: skip the traditional networking events and let's work on a better plan together for the future—for *your* future.

Don't Get Dirty with Me

When you think about "networking," how does it make you feel? If you're like many people, you might actually feel physically dirty, according to one study.[3] Researchers from Harvard Business School, the University of Toronto, and Northwestern University "hypothesized that professional networking increases feelings of inauthenticity and immorality … much more so than networking to make friends," as they report on the Harvard Business School Working Knowledge site.[4] When people are schmoozing person after person instead of seeking human connection and genuine conversation, it makes sense they start to feel a bit two-faced.

"Connection is a relationship; networking is a transaction."
—**Tim Carroll**

Those same researchers also found that networking can make low-power employees feel inauthentic and unclean. But coauthor Francesca Gino noted that high-power people know they can contribute reciprocal value, so it's important to network with something other than career goals in mind.

"If you focus on what you can offer to the relationship, it might be an important mindset to have, and remove some of those feelings of inauthenticity," said Gino, adding how the two motivational systems of prevention and promotion serve two different basic needs. "In prevention mode, you're thinking about your oughts, duties,

---

3 Tiziana Casciaro, Francesca Gino, and Maryam Kouchaki, "The Contaminating Effects of Building Instrumental Ties," *Administrative Science Quarterly* 59, no. 4 (October 6, 2014): 705–35, https://doi.org/10.1177/0001839214554990.

4 Carmen Nobel, "Professional Networking Makes People Feel Dirty," HBS Working Knowledge, February 9, 2015, https://hbswk.hbs.edu/item/professional-networking-makes-people-feel-dirty.

and obligations," she said. "In promotion mode, you're thinking about growth, advancement and accomplishments … we find that using a promotion approach helps people avoid the feelings of dirtiness that can come with professional networking."

Word Choice

With all this in mind, here's something to ponder: What if, before we do *anything* else, we agree to exchange two words for new ones. First, we agree to exchange the word "networking" with "connecting." Second, we agree to exchange the word "contacts" with "friends."

Then, what if we set your goal to "connect" with more people and build "friendships," instead of "network" more and build your "contact" list.

These shifts are subtle but will make a powerful impact on your future.

Let's agree that your new goal is to "connect" more and build "friendships" with the right people.

With that in mind, what do you do? For one, you can't be fake. Otherwise you'll spend your whole life pretending and people will see right through you. You'll be forced to talk with people you don't enjoy talking with and to do activities you hate to do. Hate golf? Don't try to meet people at country clubs and don't schedule golf meetings. Find people whom you like being around and whose friendships will both form and endure from both of you being your authentic selves. (More on this later.) Second, your mindset will shift from looking internally (collecting contacts) to externally (building friendships). As the late, great Zig Ziglar famously said, "If you go looking for a friend, you're going to find they're very scarce. If you go out to be a friend, you'll find them everywhere."

"Once you cross the threshold of a customer's personal home, your relationship changes forever. They will never fire you no matter what. They will protect you. They will defend you. They will stand behind you. They will give you a first strike, a second strike, a third strike, and a 96th strike because you took the time to go to their house, meet them and solve their problem and meet their family. And they will never forget it." —**Randy Smith**

Having taken this approach with my own life, I now go through my list of clients and business "contacts" whom I've helped and can confidently say, "[Name] has become a close friend of mine." I can also confidently say that I truly enjoy spending time with each of them and that each of them has helped me as much as I've helped them, all without me even needing to ask them for help.

The Biggest Problems with New Ways of Networking

Fortunately, social media and many other "new" ways of networking have given us alternative ways to connect. Unfortunately, they don't solve all the networking problems. Many times, they just give people other ways to become transactional, inauthentic, or rushed.

And, unlike in baseball, you only get one strike before you're out when it comes to building authentic relationships with people. With that little room for error, why in the world would anyone want to approach someone in a transactional, inauthentic, or rushed manner *anywhere*? You wouldn't. Or, at least, you *shouldn't* if you want to build the right connections.

Unfortunately, many people get this very wrong. They act as if the *platform* makes a difference, like asking for a favor on the first interaction on social media is somehow different from asking for a favor in the first sentence at a networking event. Here are some of the most common mistakes people make with the new ways of networking. Get these out of your repertoire to make room for a much better way to connect, which the rest of this book will give you.

1. Spamming People on Social Media

Imagine going into a room with 10 people you've never met before. You know nothing about their business, other than they are CEOs. Would you open with "It's great to connect with you. I hope you're doing well. I run [your business] which helps people just like you connect with more customers all around the world. In just 15 minutes, I can show you how we work. Here's my phone number. Here's my email. Here's my website. What day works best for you to get on a discovery call with me next week?"

How likely would you be to want to schedule a call with that person? Or, even better, how likely would you be to want to hire that person to get you more customers if their strategy for getting their own customers is to spam people on LinkedIn? Would you want them representing your brand?

Of course you wouldn't. Yet that's what way too many people do on social media. They request a connection on LinkedIn using some automated system or based on a search for job titles. If the connection request is accepted, they immediately follow up with an ask, in most cases asking for more of your time so they can give you a longer sales pitch.

Perhaps they get one customer for every thousand people they spam, but I can't imagine spamming 10,000 people to land 10 clients is a good long-term plan. If you're wondering why people do this, it's because some so-called gurus run around teaching people to do this as a "social selling" technique. Ugh.

2. Automating Your Asks

Sure, automation can save you a lot of time. But don't do it with your asks. For one, there's no precise "right time" to go in for an ask that applies to every relationship. Second, inauthentic, obviously cut-and-paste asks rarely work. People can see right through them.

Yet some people put together some five-email sequence that fires off with every new contact they meet. If an automated ask works, it's likely going to be with someone who is not an ideal prospect for you.

Remember, the title of this book is a call to action. We *must* save our asks when it comes to relationships and networking. Saving your asks *also* means having a more authentic mindset when you approach connection! Don't worry. I'll show you exactly what to do later in the book. First, I need to help you avoid all the things that don't work. That will free up your time and energy for bigger and better things.

3. Wasting Your Asks

We have so many opportunities these days that many people waste their asks by asking for things that don't even matter in the long run.

For example, one recent example of not wasting an ask in my life has to do with the book you're holding. Unlike most books, including my first book, you'll notice that this book has no endorsements at the front. There's nothing wrong with collecting endorsements, but endorsements are mostly about the author. I could have asked a lot of the people I feature in this book if they would endorse it, and I'm sure each of them would have. Instead, I decided to ask if I could *feature them* in the book by sharing their advice and stories in a way that helps readers become better networkers. A friend of mine describes this as "turning an ask into a give." Instead of asking them to endorse me, I give them the spotlight by featuring them. And, frankly, endorsements are overrated. Hardly anyone buys a book because of the endorsements, so using my relationship capital to ask for something that wouldn't move the needle in my life would have been a big waste.

In the end, when you waste an ask, you often end up receiving less value than you could have had you saved your asks for something that truly mattered in helping you achieve your dream. Be patient. Build the relationship.

"When you are trying to sell, the human connection—and understanding the objectives of the person you are selling to—is the piece that can make or break your pitch. The crucial part of selling anything is understanding what the person on the other side of the table wants and how whatever you are selling can help them achieve that goal. You have to know your audience." —**Lydia Fenet**

4. Getting Stalker-ish

With so much information available at our fingertips, it's very easy to cross the line between "research and persistence" and "stalking" someone. "Sometimes you can go too far with doing your research on people," warns Cary Franklin. Cary is a super close friend of mine who is also one of the best connectors I know.

He has been selling software technology for years, which is a very commoditized space. It's an industry where there are *many* salespeople who could better save their asks. Cary is an exception to that. He's one of the best connectors and salespeople I know and is a big proponent of doing the *right* amount of research.

"And then it gets into the creepy." Franklin shares a story of a peer who wanted to connect with a VP of digital, so he started researching and found she was really into meditation. He sent her a meditation book. Then he paid a B2B database for her cell phone number—and, out of the blue, just texted her a video. Her response? "Please stop." Ouch.

"His intent was good, but he was so eager to please her that he went into the creepy world," says Franklin. "When you start sending people videos on their cell phones, you've crossed the line, especially with women. And so now you're just the weirdo guy."

5. Asking Too Soon

Let's say your kid's school is running a silent auction to raise money and is looking for donated items. You recently met someone who owns a local sports memorabilia shop. They might be able to donate an autographed picture. But you only met them a few times. Is this *really* how you want to use your ask? You can each likely help each other out way more than that if you build an authentic connection. What if you *bought* a $200 autographed picture from them instead and donated it to the school yourself? You don't tell them you are buying it to donate. You just buy it. When it sells, you can reach out and let them know you donated it and it was a hit. They might tell you they would have donated it if you had asked, but the point is that you *didn't* ask. Instead, you turned your ask into a give. You gave them a sale and exposure for their business at the silent auction.

My motto is to do 30 gives before asking for anything. Focus on the long game. I allow people to ask me how they can help me before I ever make an ask. And I often politely decline their first several offers before making an ask for anything. That way, I know I'm neither wasting an ask nor asking too soon.

Spot the Askhole

Meet Carl. He's always asking for something: "Will you buy my book? Can you refer me to two people? Can you hook me up with tickets?"

Now, meet Nicole. She's always offering something: "Can I buy your book for my team? Can I refer you to two people? Can I give you these tickets?"

Which one would you rather spend time with? Which one would you support and become friends with? And which one would you recommend to a colleague?

Nicole, of course. Carl's an askhole. Anyone who goes in with more than one ask at a time is an askhole. Get rid of the askholes in your network. The best way of doing this is simply ignoring them—I promise they'll go away on their own. Also, don't be an askhole!

I wrote this book to set up the Nicoles of the world to always win—and the askholes of the world to all disappear (well, technically, not for them to disappear but to learn a better way to build connections ...).

Finding the Sweet Spot

When putting together your plan, keep in mind the concept I call the "ask continuum," which I illustrated below. On the far left, we have those who find it *very* easy to go in for the ask (these are often askholes). On the far right, we have those who *never* go in for the ask or feel bad doing it (they tend to let asks—and opportunities—pass them by).

Where do you tend to fall on the ask continuum? If you're too far to the left, you might ask too soon or too much. It might be time to save some more of your asks. If you tend to fall on the right, you might have a lot of relationship capital built up. It might be time for you to work on asking a bit sooner. The sweet spot is right in the center, making meaningful asks at the appropriate time. (Don't worry, the rest of this book will help you end up right in the sweet spot.)

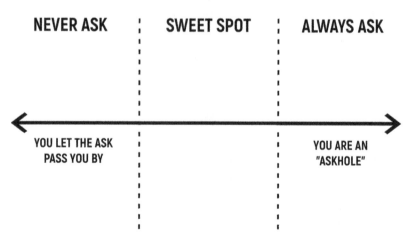

NEVER ASK	SWEET SPOT	ALWAYS ASK
YOU LET THE ASK PASS YOU BY		YOU ARE AN "ASKHOLE"

TL;DR

Quit wasting your time going to "networking" events and instead focus on making connections *every week*! Save your asks and watch your business and network grow.

Make the Connection

- Create a "purpose statement." Everyone around me knows mine: "to inspire and connect." What's yours? Once you realize it, you can start working toward it—one small step at a time.
- Make it a goal to meet a certain number of new people every week.
- Disregard status or "rank" when connecting.
- In networking, you get just one strike. You have very little room for error. You only get one ask of everyone around you—*save your ask*.

CHAPTER 2:
You're Playing Small Ball

*"Shoot for the moon. Even if you miss,
you'll land among the stars."*
–Norman Vincent Peale

Otoro tartare. Sake aioli. Aburi hotate.

These are just a few of the menu items at Umi, one of Atlanta's (and arguably, the Southeast's) most exclusive restaurants. Yes, the Japanese cuisine is spectacular. But it's the grand vision and attention to detail from owner Farshid Arshid that have made this a "come-hither sushi den," as one reviewer called it, and lured celebrities like Sir Anthony Hopkins and Gwyneth Paltrow. Getting a reservation at Umi can feel like winning the Super Bowl of dining experiences.

This is nowhere near where Farshid would be had he not learned to think big—really big. As a five-year-old boy in Iran, he imagined himself in politics. "That's all I could think about," recalls Farshid, who then realized at age seven he had a knack for both big ideas and taking action on those ideas. "I would always take action," he emphasizes when he recalls some of the reasons he separated himself from the millions of people whose ideas die inside them.

In 1981, the Iranian revolution pushed him to boarding school in Switzerland. But he wasn't like the other students, who sped around in Lamborghinis or enjoyed the luxury of having their own full-time drivers. Farshid didn't have anything close to that level of wealth. In many ways, he was a misfit at that school. But he was hundreds of miles away from home, so he had to figure out a way to make genuine connections with classmates with whom he seemingly had little in common. Even worse, his family ended up losing what relatively little wealth they had during an oil crisis, leaving him completely unable to even keep up with a group of kids whose common denominators consisted of pedigree and wealth.

Without wealth or pedigree to find a common connection, Farshid discovered another currency that made other students genuinely interested in spending time with him: his athleticism. He was a talented athlete—something many of his wealthier classmates desired but could not attain.

Fortunately for Farshid, he loved playing sports, so he would enjoy using his athleticism to build connections. He also loved the business of sports. He loved everything about it. He soon found that three other passions of his—fashion, food, and music—gave him authentic means of connection that didn't require abundant wealth.

Finding four passions many other people shared early on in life has continued to serve Farshid well. Not only did it help him make genuine connections with people during his childhood but it also helped him build businesses as an adult that were fueled by his genuine passion and not by a pursuit of money alone.

"I have never, never, ever in my life done anything just for money," says Farshid, who became one of the country's top restaurateurs after 17 years in the music industry. Why is that important? Because it is easy to quit when things get tough—especially when you pursue something just for the money. But that's often the worst time to quit. Tough times are a sign that you are pushing yourself further than you have before. They are signs of growth. They are signs that you are expanding your comfort zone. They are signs that you are trying to do more or bigger things than you typically do in a day, week, or even a year. Things get tough because you're breaking out from your "ordinary" in some important way.

"We all fear thinking big and facing failure. But every hardship we face takes us to a new place," says Farshid. "I compare it to a video game," he says. "If you're on the first level of a video game, it's super easy. But then as you get to higher and higher levels, it gets harder and harder, and then more stuff starts coming at you, and it gets faster. You might pass Level 1 right away, and then you hit Level 10 and fail 500 times. But after 500, you go to Level 11, and Level 11 is paradise."

"Adversity is part of the journey. Nothing happens to you. It's all happening for you." —**Alex Molden**

In practice, too many people don't aim high enough. They set goals that don't require them to push through tough times. In Farshid's terms, they set "Level 10" goals. Many of them assume Level 10 is as good as it gets for them. But paradise is often just one tough time past Level 10. So why set such small goals? Set goals that force you to go through tough times. And when you push through and hit paradise, set new and bigger goals that help you achieve even greater goals and impact even more people in the world.

Your Brain on Big Goals

Farshid's experience might seem unattainable to many people. They hear how he reached the top of multiple industries and think he had an unfair advantage. The truth is he just aimed at different targets than what most people do. He didn't just want to "work in music," he wanted to make it to the top of the music industry. He didn't want to just "be involved in tennis," he set a goal of rising to the top of the tennis world. And he didn't want to just "open a restaurant," he aimed for opening a destination restaurant. He set big goals. That's why he achieved big things.

I played soccer as a kid. Small ball. Small goals. And now, I meet people every day who are still playing small ball, with small goals to match.

Research shows that we can actually rewire our brain—and become incredibly successful—by simply setting ambitious goals. In a study published in *Behavioral and Cognitive Neuroscience Reviews*,[5] researchers found that goal setting alters the neuroplasticity of our brains so we're primed to achieve that goal. As study author Rebecca Compton writes, "First, emotional significance is evaluated preattentively by a subcortical circuit involving the amygdala; and second, stimuli deemed emotionally significant are given priority in the competition for access to selective attention.

---

5   Rebecca J. Compton, "The Interface between Emotion and Attention: A Review of Evidence from Psychology and Neuroscience," *Behavioral and Cognitive Neuroscience Reviews* 2, no. 2 (June 1, 2003): 115–29, https://doi.org/10.1177 /1534582303002002003.

This process involves bottom-up inputs from the amygdala as well as top-down influences from frontal lobe regions involved in goal setting and maintaining representations in working memory."

Put more simply, our amygdalas—which typically determine primitive fight vs. flight responses and control our emotions—can also help us determine how important our goals are to us. Our frontal lobes, which do the hard work, figure out exactly what the goal entails. They work together to keep us focused on, say, finding a new star in the galaxy or providing clean water for one million children in India.

And here's what I really love about this research. We only know how to do this when we determine our own goals—when we tap into our own currencies. As Geoffrey James writes in *Inc.* magazine, "The brain-changing power of goal setting works only when it taps into the characteristics of the goal-setter's individual brain."[6]

As superhuman as it may seem, our brains can physically adapt to help us complete goals—but only when we're serious about them.

Three Things at a Time

I'm not a *huge* fan of very specific long-term goals because I believe our heads and our hearts as well as the world around us evolve too fast for those to stay relevant. Instead, I like to envision more directional long-term goals, such as financial independence, while working where your passions, professions, and talents intersect. Then, I like to focus on the small goals that keep

---

6   Geoffrey James, "What Goal-Setting Does to Your Brain and Why It's Spectacularly Effective," *Inc.*, Inc.com, October 23, 2019, https://www.inc.com/geoffrey-james/what-goal-setting-does-to-your-brain-why-its-spectacularly-effective.html.

us focused and cranking toward building the momentum in the right direction. (Have I mentioned that I'm actually addicted to momentum now?)

It's simpler than it seems to achieve bigger goals than you ever imagined with this approach. I call doing "three things at a time" every day. We can pursue only a handful of things, and what works best for me is to write down the three things that I'm going after that day. It might be the name of someone I'm determined to meet or a company I want to land as a client for my ad agency, but I just write down three simple things to focus on each day. The simplicity of this allows me to stay focused.

For example, I've been advising a web developer and marketing executive named Justin Hegwood for a while. When we first discussed his sales strategy, I learned that he was sending out mass LinkedIn messages, basically blanketing Atlanta with pitches to build them a website. "*Everyone* is selling websites," I told him. "If you want to stand out, you need to be more than just a web developer. Stop blanketing Atlanta and get more strategic."

He grew up in south Georgia and has a thick Southern accent. I knew he'd have much better luck in areas and industries that would want the authentic Justin. He began focusing on manufacturing, construction, and small businesses like dentistry outside of metro Atlanta. "Start courting those three areas," I told him. "And if they're not working out, find another top three." You should always have a batter's box you can turn to for your three things at a time, and once you make that initial connection, you're able to go deeper. Within each of those categories, there's a decision-maker you can meet with a warm introduction.

I challenged Justin to find three people in each category and work backward from there. Sure enough, by focusing on authentic outreach to just three leads at a time, Justin began making more and better connections. Soon enough, his schedule started filling up. (If you want to see some of the work Justin and his team at The Artist Evolution do, check out www.christuff.me.)

Follow the Breadcrumbs

When Candace Nelson whipped up the hugely successful Sprinkles cupcake company in 2005, she "followed the bread-crumbs," as she calls it, to completely pivot her career. After graduating from Wesleyan, taking a prestigious investment job, and then working in a San Francisco start-up during the dot-com boom of the 1990s, she suddenly found herself unemployed when the bubble burst. "I'd done all the right things, from A to Z, and there I was on the couch with no job prospects," she recalls. "I thought, *How does this happen? I did everything I was supposed to do.* For the first time in my life, I basically did nothing."

She watched *The Martha Stewart Show*. She watched *Oprah*. And when the pity party ended, she started thinking about what she *wanted* to do instead of what she felt like she *should* do. Surrounded by the food celebrities of San Francisco, she was inspired to go to pastry school "thinking this is a fun hobby," says Candace, who tested it out for a few months and discovered she loved it. "I thought, *Oh, I've been working so hard for so many hours. Start-up hours are so brutal. Do I really need to spend so much of my life working?*" she recalls. "How miserable is it to spend most of your life doing something you don't like doing?"

Right out of pastry school, she started making cakes and cupcakes out of her kitchen. A modest start, for sure. After achieving modest success, she and her husband, Charles, who had also always wanted to be an entrepreneur, realized she was cooking up something with major potential. Cupcakes were becoming a trend in the wedding scene, but they were still shoved in plastic clamshells in the supermarkets, fit for a kid's lunchbox and not much else.

While many people would want to get a small piece of the cupcake market, Candace decided to go bigger and completely reinvent the humble cupcake. "I thought, *Here's something everyone in this country loves, but they don't think about it anymore because they think it's just a kid's treat. But if we can make it sort of a grown-up thing and it's elegant, then we can kind of move into a whole new market.*"

And that's when Sprinkles was born. By aiming big, Candace looked differently at the cupcake and turned her humble kitchen baking hustle into the first cupcake chain, earning millions of dollars and landing on the very show Candace had watched while considering how to network her way back into business: *Oprah*.

After aiming big, of course, Candace had to figure out how to achieve such an audacious goal. So what did she do? "I call it following the breadcrumbs," explains Candace, who had no Facebook or Instagram leads when she started Sprinkles. When they moved to L.A., she and Charles had no network. "But it became this burning desire, this idea that I became obsessed with and I really believed in. Even in spite of the fact that everybody thought it was a stupid idea, I couldn't get it out of my head. And there were times during the process where it didn't look like it was going to happen. We couldn't find the supplies or the locations. But I thought, *I am not going to be able to live with myself if I don't pursue it. I don't care if I fall flat on my face; I just have to do it.*"

Candace began by looking in the phone book for restaurant suppliers and talking one West Hollywood contact into selling her chocolate. He then introduced her to an equipment supplier who knew about locations coming on the market. A friend from their banking days introduced her and Charles to the friend's mother, who owned a bakery in L.A. and gave them information on equipment and hiring. "We would go and sit at her table during her quiet time of day, and she would feed us milk and cookies and talk about the business," says Candace. "You establish a relationship with one person, and they lead you to somebody else. So much of it is not burning bridges, being a kind and decent person so you can reach out to anyone you come across throughout your life. And generally, people are wanting to help."

"You will get all you want in life if you help enough other people get what they want." —**Zig Ziglar**

One of the key takeaways of Candace's story is that, although she ended up building a "cupcake empire," she did so one small step at a time. She simply followed the breadcrumbs toward her big vision for making cupcakes a grown-up thing and stayed tenacious and resilient enough for this outcome to become a byproduct of ruthlessly pursuing one of her passions.

Doll Clothes Anyone?

One of my favorite examples of someone creating a business out of a niche passion comes from a couple named Jason and Cinnamon Miles. Cinnamon had been sewing doll clothes for their kids' American Girl dolls. She made beautiful clothes. Over time, others started to notice and asked if she could make clothes for them too. Over time, her clothes became so popular that she was selling them online and on eBay for pretty good money. Demand got so high that Cinnamon couldn't keep up, so Jason and Cinnamon needed to adjust their plans and aim much higher than simply selling doll clothes online.

Instead of continuing to sell clothes, Jason and Cinnamon decided to sell digital versions of the clothing patterns so people could create their own versions of Cinnamon's designs. Like the clothing, demand for Cinnamon's designs became incredibly popular. Thousands of people all around the world ordered designs. In shifting from selling clothes to selling designs, Jason and Cinnamon were able to achieve limitless scale and they've crushed it!

In just a matter of months of selling designs, Jason and Cinnamon were able to create both the time and the revenue to help fund an orphanage in West Africa. They have since grown that heart for helping into an organization called Sew Powerful, a registered 501(c)(3) organization through which they help people in need all around the world. Yes, "the riches *are* in the niches."

Go from SMART to SMARTEST Goals

A lifelong animal lover, Jasen Trautwein studied zoology and animal biology at the University of Texas at Austin and worked as a veterinarian before founding his own company, Pathway Vet Alliance—and selling it for more than $2 billion. Yes, his passion for dogs and cats became a multibillion-dollar business.

How did he turn a passion for animals into a multibillion-dollar business? By aiming big. "As the entrepreneur, I was the rate-limiting step in *my* vision for the teams," says Jasen, explaining how he inadvertently held his employees back from achieving their visions and taking the company to greater heights. "I always thought my job was to support my team and provide the highest level of service and care to our clients and patients. I spent all day focusing on the little things that made for positive experiences at my business. Over time, however, I realized that approach was selling my team short, and they could achieve much more than I was allowing them to do." At that point, Jasen shifted from working in the business and on the business to working on himself. He got very specific about establishing a big vision for the company and set focused goals to help him and his team build momentum toward his big vision.

Although I'm not a big long-term goals guy, I do know we can achieve big things if we set a series of short-term goals that help us build momentum. However, we need to avoid common goal-setting traps that cause us to fail. And one of those traps is the common "SMART" goal-setting strategy that way too many people tout. Why? Because SMART goals really only work on paper. Not only that, but they fail to take into account whether achieving that goal improves your life in a way that matters to you. You know what happens when you achieve a goal that doesn't matter to you? You're miserable, like my friend whose lifelong dream was to become a lawyer, only to find himself miserable after just a few years in the profession.

With just a few simple tweaks, however, we can turn SMART goals into the SMARTEST goals and help you set goals that actually improve your life. Specifically, SMART goals are goals that are

- Specific
- Measurable
- Achievable

- Relevant
- Time-bound

While seemingly helpful, SMART goals fail to take into account the human element of goal setting. Your goals need to acknowledge that an actual human with limited time, seemingly unlimited responsibilities, and a whole host of other factors needs to actually do the work to achieve the goal. For those reasons, I encourage people to turn their SMART goals into the SMART-EST possible goals by adding three more letters, "EST," to the acronym if they really want to make goals stick:

- **Exciting**: You need to enjoy doing the work.
- **Seasonally Appropriate**: Can you do it at this time? What's the "seasonally appropriate" version of your goal? If you're 60, you're likely not going to be an Olympic weight lifter—but you could compete in a 60-plus weight lifting competition.
- **Transformational**: Will achieving your goal transform your life in a meaningful way? Or at least make it more enjoyable?

Let's look at some examples of the SMARTEST goals in practice.

First, meet my friend Allison, who is a partner at one of the top law firms in the U.S., specializing in employment law. After attending one of my lectures on the importance of passion, purpose, and profession all overlapping, she realized she'd been neglecting her own passion for physical fitness and well-being. Her business development efforts had been more "standard" in the legal world, being intentional about networking but not intentionally combining her networking with her passions. My lecture inspired her to adjust her efforts and intentionally pursue clients for her law firm that would allow her to combine her passion for physical fitness and well-being with her legal practice. She started by reaching out to a number of physical fitness and well-being brands, including Nike and Peloton, and has begun building a relationship with Nike. Allison is now actively pursuing even more opportunities to combine her law practice and networking efforts with her personal passions. This is a great example of making sure "exciting" is part of your SMARTEST goals.

Then there's my former colleague—we'll call him Paul—who lost his marketing job during the COVID-19 crisis. He wanted to start his own company but was going through a divorce and needed a more predictable income during this season of life, so he adjusted his goal to land a job where he could stay with his kids in Kentucky. With this new focus, he landed a job with a California company that allowed him to work remotely. Paul accepted happily and achieved a perfect seasonally appropriate version of his goal to further his marketing career.

Small Transformations That Lead to Big Change

When I talk with people about SMARTEST goals, many people get intimidated by the idea of goals needing to be "transformational." Although I agree that it can sound intimidating, it's really just about asking yourself whether achieving your goal will add or take away stress from your life.

For example, I feel 50/50 about my Roomba. Sure, it's convenient, but I find myself constantly fixing it. It definitely doesn't take away significant stress from my life. But birdseed that brings beautiful winged creatures to my backyard? Candles that fill my dream home with calming and uplifting fragrances? A Vero Water machine that delivers perfectly carbonated H_2O at the perfect temperature with a tiny tug of the tap? These are all things that take away stress, so they're worthy investments.

When applying this principle to goal setting, just remember that transformational can be a small thing. So instead of getting overwhelmed by setting lofty goals, such as landing Nike as an account for your agency, consider creating smaller goals that build toward your larger goals, such as landing your first sports apparel brand to build your résumé.

Going Big

Until recently, my brother Alex worked for a private life insurance brokerage firm in New York City. He helped land me on the front page of the *Wall Street Journal* when he spoofed my video of proposing to my wife, Julie. So he's got a great sense of humor and a great sense of people to work with. One of them is Aaron Abrahms.

Alex told me a story when I was looking for him to connect me with the best salespeople. Aaron, Alex said, was watching the Super Bowl one year and realized he had never had a meeting with either team's owner. By the end of the game, he had meetings set up with both owners. Clearly, he knew how to go big in his goals—and achieve them. I had to meet with him.

"Connecting genuinely with other people is like a puzzle and I get an adrenaline rush from it. So when I get a response like—'Yes, we'll take a meeting' or 'Yes, we'll work with you (or partner with you),'—I really get a lot of pleasure out of that." —**Alexandra Wilkis Wilson**

Every year, Aaron will set up super exclusive cocktail parties for some of these elusive high-net-worth individuals and managers of family offices. What's different about his approach is he doesn't hang a banner with the name of his company or give an awkward sales pitch. He just brings these people together in different big cities and allows them to meet and talk to one another. One of the most important things Aaron taught me was the idea that being the catalyst for allowing people to network with others similar to themselves is your first win.

PROSPECT NAME	1ST MEETING	2ND MEETING	3RD MEETING	FINAL PITCH	CLIENT
BILL GATES	BILL GATES	BILL GATES	BILL GATES	BILL GATES	BILL GATES
JEFF BEZOS	JEFF BEZOS	JEFF BEZOS			
CARLISLE GROUP					
MARK ZUCKERBERG					
GWYNETH PALTROW					
LEBRON					

"The hardest part of sales is staying in touch," says Aaron. "You have to be genuinely helpful to prospects." Don't just put people on an email distribution list and hope it will work out. Be organized and have a good memory. Memorize or note the names of their kids, their hobbies, the trips they are taking, etc., so you can pick back up where you left off next time you speak with them.

"Never be the first to talk and always listen first—the more they talk, the better it is," says Aaron. "Be an interesting person. Read books or listen to podcasts to become more interesting as every successful person is a lifelong learner."

Keeping Score

A huge part of setting and achieving goals is keeping track of them, and there are a gazillion tools out there to help you. Personally, I rely on a system developed by "The Great Eight," a mini-mastermind group of guys I belong to, which I will talk about more in part 2.

Our collective goal is to help each other become better men by being better husbands, fathers, and businesspeople. We essentially break down success into three main parts: personal, professional, and family.

Every month when we meet, we check in and score ourselves in each part on a scale from 1 to 10. This way not only can we rely on the others to call out any big shifts from one month to the next but it also acts as a practical gut check to our emotional selves. Giving myself a monthly score allows me to track my progress and hold myself accountable for improving how I perform in three important categories.

Keeping score is helpful on more specific levels too. For example, Aaron Abrahms inspired me to create a system for connections. I now have a giant whiteboard in my office where on the far left I list all the organizations and people I want to meet with: the "prospect list." Next is a column noting when I set a meeting up with that person or organization, followed by another column marking a "formal credentials" meeting. The fourth column records when we pitch an idea or campaign, and the final column is "Won as a Client." I give myself six weeks to make the connection work. If not, I remove the name from the board and put it on an inactive list.

Write a List to Generate Wins and Momentum

"A person can feel stuck at any stage in their life, at any age, having achieved tons of success or just starting out," says Alexandra Wilkis Wilson, serial entrepreneur and cofounder of Gilt Groupe. "I'm very goal-oriented. So every time I get stuck, or I feel down about myself or unmotivated, I know it's because my next goal isn't clear to me. That's not to say I've achieved every goal—that's not the case at all. But I get adrenalized when I embark on frantic list-making with very clear goals in mind. The list is my tactical approach for how to achieve the goal."

Once you begin tackling your list with *action*, the momentum accelerates, and you can get closer to realizing even bigger goals.

Decide Who You Want to Be

"Most of the time it's that one thing that takes you down to your core," says Alex Molden, a former NFL player who's now a performance coach for Nike. "Who do you want to be? What do you want to be? What gives you joy? And what relationships do you need to make?"

Many times, people aim too low with their goals because they have a limited view of what's possible. They think there's something wrong with them, their background, or their circumstances that prevent them from achieving big things. To them, there's a limit to the success they can achieve. It's understandable.

When you're juggling all of life's demands, it can be hard to envision yourself achieving big goals. For the time being, however,

I want you to suspend disbelief. I want you to decide who you want to be with the assumption that you can achieve it. You might not know how just yet. And you might need to develop some new skills or uplevel your network. But let's assume for the moment that you can achieve big things.

Decide who you want to be three years from now. Assume that everything goes well between now and then. Who do you want to be? What do you want to be doing? What does your life look like? Later in this book, I'll help you get there. For now, I just want you to aim big. Envision a life three years from now that you love.

Aim big. Even if you miss, you will almost inevitably end up achieving bigger things than if you aim too low and hit your goal every time.

TL;DR

Start creating a system of measurable and accountable goals. Find a crew or mastermind to share your goals with and focus on a few small wins. Never stop moving forward—progress is where joy lives!

Make the Connection

- Make your long-term goals adaptable so you can pivot along the way.
- Break big goals into smaller goals.
- Join a small group or mastermind to hold you accountable to your goals.
- Be patient with your timelines for connection—it takes time to develop a deep connection.
- Write your goals on a whiteboard that you can revisit *every* day.

- Create a system for multiple touch points, using a white-board or software.
- Be the one who can bring like-minded clients together in a social setting or activity so you act as the catalyst to them all meeting.
- Make sure these are your goals, not somebody else's.
- Write down the three things you're going to do each day.
- Look at your list of goals and make sure they are SMART-EST goals: Are your goals exciting, seasonally appropriate, and transformational? If not, write a new list.
- Visit ChrisTuff.me/Resources for more help setting long-term vision and shorter-term goals.

CHAPTER 3:

Your Currency

You know what's wrong with traditional networking. You're thinking bigger than before. You're aiming higher than you have in the past. Now you take inventory of the best tools you have at your disposal to work with: your current networking currencies.

Remember, your currencies are all the things about you that other people find valuable. It can be access to events, a talent, or even an ability to make people feel important. For example, a friend of mine used to be a lawyer at a large law firm in New York City. When he first started working there, the office was run by a guy named Bill.

Bill was a talented lawyer with a long track record of success. As managing partner, he needed to manage all the lawyers and office administration on top of his legal practice. It might not surprise you to learn that it's impossible to make dozens of high-profile lawyers happy. But while Bill wasn't able to keep everyone happy, my friend remembers to this day—nearly two decades later—that one thing that made Bill someone people wanted to be around was that he *always* made people feel important. "When you went to Bill to help solve a problem, you might not have always gotten your way," my friend told me. "But you *always* left his office feeling better than when you went in."

The ability for Bill to make people feel important, and to do so authentically, was something that helped Bill build long-term relationships and rise up the corporate ladder at one of the most prestigious law firms in the world.

So when you start thinking of your currencies, expand your mindset. You don't need season tickets to the Atlanta Braves or New York Yankees. You don't need to be able to get reservations at Umi on short notice. But *everyone* has at least *one* networking currency that other people value: what they are paid to do.

Put simply, if someone pays you to perform a task, they are telling you that you have value. If you sell software, your networking currency is your ability to understand and sell that software. If you design pools for people, your currency is pool design. If you install kitchen cabinets, your currency is everything related to the skills and talent it takes to be a master craftsperson.

Everyone also has subcurrencies too: additional hobbies and interests that other people are interested in but that you are not currently exploiting for your benefit (financially or otherwise).

When you don't love what you are paid to do, your subcurrency can help drive you and your networking. But your main currency is still what your company pays you to do. Over time, you can develop your subcurrencies enough to replace your current currency as the primary driver of your networking progress. Until then, most of your networking results will come from using your existing currency and connections to help others.

What does this look like? Take Ken Hannaman, for example.

Ken rose from humble beginnings to his current position as an executive at Arby's. He has walked in the shoes and lived the lives of many of the people he now leads. He began as a minimum wage employee in the restaurant industry and worked his way up to his current position.

For someone in Ken's position, you might think that his primary currency that fuels his success is his influence and connections as an executive of a large company. If you asked Ken, however, he would credit his continued success to his ability to relate to and challenge people at all levels to continuously perform and improve. Ken developed that currency working his way up the ladder in the restaurant industry, transitioning his currency from hard work and dedication to improvement to the ability to help others do the same.

"Whether they are entry-level or senior-level team members, I see my currency as having the ability to challenge others to live their best lives alongside me on our personal and professional life paths," Ken shared with me.

Was Ken passionate about working hard for minimum wage when he just started? I doubt it. But his passion for helping people live their best lives oozed through the Zoom screen when I interviewed him for the book.

If you look in the mirror and see that you are *not* passionate about your currency, don't freak out. We can evolve that currency in a responsible way without burning the boats just like Ken did. He didn't accept working hard for minimum wage his entire career. He slowly demonstrated the ability to relate with and lead others as he worked his way to the top of the corporate world, eventually becoming more known for his ability to lead others than his ability to do the day-to-day work himself.

As we'll discuss, you'll be creating your "passions" soon enough. These passions will also help you increase the size of your network and your ability to "race to the middle" in finding common passion points in networking (more to come on that).

Start with the Life You Want

If you're having trouble identifying your currency, think back to the life you imagined at the end of chapter 2. What did you envision yourself doing? What you are looking to build in the future could give you a hint about a currency buried deep inside you just waiting to be developed.

Forget about the past or the present. What is your ideal future? What is it that you're *truly* passionate about? At the core of everything I do is my purpose "to inspire and connect." Everyone around me knows my purpose statement. I also know that it's my absolute passion to inspire people to realize their dreams and passions through work. Define your purpose, put a stake in the ground, and make sure it rolls off your tongue at every turn. But you have to dream big and then break that big dream down into smaller pieces.

"What was I born to do?" asks Dan Miller in *48 Days to the Work (and Life) You Love: Preparing for the New Normal*. "What would be my greatest contribution to others? What do I really love to do (and when I'm doing it, time just flies by)? What are the recurring themes that I find myself drawn to? How do I want to be remembered?"

These are some of the best words I've read regarding our ruthless pursuit of passions, and I highly recommend reading Dan's work for more advice on finding work that is meaningful, purposeful, and profitable.

"You have to have a lot of passion for what you are doing, because it is so hard ... if you don't, any rational person would give up."
—**Steve Jobs**

Dan Miller helps people find (and monetize) their passions. His recent email to potential clients clearly lays out the payoff for pursuing your passion:

Imagine with me for a moment that you were able to start a side business around something that you love and within six months be generating $4,800 a month.

What would that mean for you and your family?

If you're working a full-time job and making $100,000 a year, the $57,600 a year you would generate from the side business you love would be more than 50% of what you're making full time.

This gives you the freedom to:

1. Keep your full-time job and your side business and give your family the extra income you need to do what you want in life

- *Pay off debt*
- *Save for the future*
- *Buy a home*
- *Afford a great family experience together*
- *Allow your spouse to stay home with the kids and/or pursue something they love*
- *Save for another rainy day like we have had recently*
- *And more!*

2. Quit your full-time job. If you are making $4,800/month just working 15 hours per week in your side business, just imagine what you can make when you start working 40 hours per week.

3. Be creative and do the things you want to do in life, perhaps working out new arrangements with your full-time employer. It's a lot easier to do when you have your side business and the confidence that you already have that momentum.

I'm here to tell you that this isn't just something to dream about over your 30-minute lunch break or while you're stuck in rush hour traffic.

It is really possible.

I had the fortune of meeting Dan at his home where several members of my mastermind were gathering for a weekend. We asked him about the philosophy that life should be a ruthless pursuit of passions. He said he believed in it wholeheartedly (and his book *48 Days to the Work (and Life) You Love* was one of the first books that brought the concept to market).

We toured Dan's property and then entered his office, which is lined with books and artwork. After our long conversation about the ruthless pursuit of passions, I thought this would be a perfect opportunity to ask him to show me examples of people who turned their passions into their professions.

"Let me tell you about that painting," said Dan, as he pointed to a painting of what looked like a modernist interpretation of a saxophone. "A preacher came to me, frustrated that he was in the wrong profession. He was unfulfilled. He wasn't passionate about it." After working with Dan, they discovered his passion for painting. Now, the preacher's work is displayed and sold in all of the top galleries throughout the U.S., and the painting that hangs in Dan's office is worth tens of thousands of dollars.

Getting Ready to Use Your Currency

With even a rough idea about what currencies you have now and the ones you want to develop, invest a combination of time and money into developing your currency and connecting with people who value you and what you are looking to build.

For example, you can take very affordable online courses on sites like Coursera.com and Udemy.com that help you develop any number of skills. On Coursera, colleges and universities submit online courses you can take for free or earn a certificate for a small fee. On Udemy, you can learn almost anything from thousands of independent educators. And you can even search for premium online courses from independent publishers with experience and connections they are willing to share for a fraction of what it would cost to go back to school for even one semester.

Investing in online courses is one of my favorite ways to test currencies and see if you truly love them with very low risk. If you learn from the course that you have no interest in developing a particular skill, you've lost very little time and money. Taking online courses differentiates you in the networking world as someone willing to invest time and money into their personal and professional growth while also creating new passion points and areas of expertise.

For example, if you're obsessed with coffee, take a course on the ins and outs of coffee, or coffee roasting, or any other number of related topics. If you love content writing, you could get a writing certificate from a highly respected college on Coursera pretty easily.

In addition to courses, I highly recommend hiring a coach or joining a mastermind group to give you personalized guidance, support, and accountability as you network. I'll talk more about these people in the next part when I talk about the people you need to surround yourself with. But the point, for this chapter, is that you can develop your currency and get used to using it to help others pretty easily with the right coach or mastermind group in your corner.

Read every book you can get your hands on that covers your topic. (See if the author of your favorite one offers coaching or a mastermind. You might be surprised how many do.)

Never stop investing time and money in developing your currencies. The more you do, the more valuable it will become. Invest in higher-level courses and masterminds.

Don't Quit Your Day Job

A friend of mine, whom we'll call John, was the head of all operations for a hypergrowth consumer products company. This company grew rapidly and had one the fastest growing products in all of Target. One day John called me and said, "Chris, I'm so burned out and I'm looking for something new. I saw a job as a recruiter at Spanx; do you think you could help me get an interview?"

My immediate response was something to the effect of, "John, no one can do what you do—you know how to deal with worldwide supply chains, logistics, and stuff I don't even know how to pronounce. You know how to get stuff shipped all over the world at a moment's notice. Your *currency* is in high demand at tons of companies! Also, I hate to tell you this, but you're underqualified for a position as a recruiter because your *currency* has nothing to do with recruiting; and, even if you get the position, which is unlikely, that would be three levels too low for your background. If you do this, you'll make the wrong move for a position you likely won't get because you're just not a good fit. *Instead*, you should embrace your currency to get in the door at companies that can allow you to move laterally toward your passion and interests."

I then suggested to John that, in order to make the right moves, he should aim to meet two new people every day (this is aggressive, to most I say two a week). I gave him his first handful of meetings out of my contacts with people who I felt would value his currency. It was about six months later that John called me. He said, "Chris, that was so much fun meeting all the people. I just landed at my new company from a connection who came from your friend Tommy Breedlove, and it's in line with my currency!" How cool is that? John almost sacrificed all of the growth and expertise that he'd acquired for a short-term gain. He also would have wasted his ask getting an introduction from me at Spanx and caused me to waste my ask at Spanx getting him an interview for a position that wasn't a good fit for him.

TL;DR

Currency is the backbone of your career and your ability to network effectively. Identify it, embrace it, and start evolving by pursuing some of your side passions.

Make the Connection
- Identify your currency and write it down to revisit.
- Ask yourself, "What was I born to do?"
- Take courses to better hone your currency and evolve some of your other interests.
- *Do not* be tempted to ditch your currency for a hobby or interest too early.

PART 2:

YOUR PEOPLE

CHAPTER 4:

Supporters and Super-Connectors

You know what fires up Randy Smith? Flooring. Yes. Flooring.

Every day, he's fired up about flooring because he's impacting thousands of lives through the services and products of the company he founded with his father in 1983, Heritage Flooring. And he will be the first to admit that the flooring business failed to feel like a passion at the time.

He was motivated by money, pure and simple. "Money-motivated is a wonderful thing because I don't think there's enough of it anymore," says Randy. So making money was Randy's original passion, which turned into something else altogether as he entered the world of entrepreneurialism. It started when he was a kid, he says, watching his dad deal with the ups and downs of owning a small business. "Some years he was taking us to Europe in the summer, and some years he was cutting the lawn in the summer," says Randy, who at first didn't think his dad had a "real" job until he started buying second homes, motorcycles, and more when Randy was 16.

In high school, Randy started his own landscaping business and also started building the relationships and reputation that would send him to success. From the beginning, he had a knack for knocking on just the right doors to build an authentic and highly supportive network. It really kicked in when he was 30 years old and flew out to California to find a mentor who would change his life forever.

This chapter is dedicated to all the people who are going to support your ruthless pursuit of passions and to all the super-connectors who will plug you into the switchboard of life how *you* want to live it.

Your Support Network

Research shows that social support is critical in our career searches as college students,[7] and it's no different for adults.

"My career trajectory and success are 95 percent attributable to sponging up everything I could from people that were more established, more developed, and better than me (at the time), and applying what I picked up along the way to everything moving forward," says Sean Reardon, Global Chief Operating Officer and US Chief Executive Officer of MiQ, a massive programmatic media company. "I worked with awesome people my whole career."

You may feel ready for the second part of this chapter—connecting with the super-connectors. But the super-connectors have

---

7   Robert W. Lent et al., "Social–Cognitive Predictors of Career Exploration and Decision-Making: Longitudinal Test of the Career Self-Management Model.," *Journal of Counseling Psychology* 66, no. 2 (March 2019): 184–94, https://doi. org/10.1037/cou0000307.

been practicing patience, which is one of the key virtues of saving your asks. The first step is identifying your existing currencies. And then it's where does that line up to your own evolving passions and your purpose? That's going to dictate the other potential networking opportunities you will be able to pursue using passions that are currencies you're not currently known for. As you're creating this momentum and motion with a new passion, continue utilizing your existing currencies to build relationships until your new currencies build their own momentum. Only after your new currency builds its own momentum and becomes more powerful than your old currency can you shift your networking focus to your new currency. That's a practice of patience.

Start with Just One Person

You only need one person to help you reach all your personal and professional goals because that person is going to help spark your passion and your lifelong, ruthless pursuit of it. Maybe that person is someone who went *after* it and inspired you to do the same. Maybe it's your boss, a member of your mastermind, or a mentor. Maybe it's the person on your team who's in a totally different industry now. No matter what, they're a personified version of your North Star, guiding you. Use them as a sounding board as you pursue your own passion—they will help tell you what you *need* to hear instead of what you *want* to hear.

"I'm the only one who believed in my vision. And that's okay. But I had to kind of create this moat around me that separates me from everybody else. I had to be able to hold a "fly-higher-than-and-above everybody else" flag. And that flag was going to be entirely representative of the people I surround myself with. And I wasn't going to get there just by people that are going to help me in my current occupation." —**Dan Scalia**

<hr>

When I first met this one guy, for example, we were both part of a study abroad program in London and both studying digital marketing. Our flats were right next to each other, and we became friends, along with a budding magician and a fashion designer. (It was an eclectic group.) When this friend told me he wanted to get into comedy, I was surprised. I didn't find him all that funny. But we all went to an open mic event at a dark-lit London pub. And he wasn't funny *at all*. We all joined him in drinking his sorrows away with a few pints.

About three years later, he emailed me about a show he was going to be doing at the famous Georgia Theatre in Athens. I thought, *Maybe he's onto something.*

And he was. He was (and still is …) Aziz Ansari, who's gone on to create and star in some of the most successful comedies of our generation, including *Parks and Rec,* and has even hosted the MTV Video Music Awards.

I started, in some ways, with Aziz Ansari. Because seeing him ruthlessly pursue his passion for comedy—seeing him going from completely un-funny to downright hilarious—showed me the little passions I could begin to build toward my currency of connecting people.

There's also stuff you were *born to do* and stuff that you are just interested in doing—Aziz Ansari is a good example of the latter.

Now, after years of networking, I know exactly the type of person to start with. It will not be Aziz Ansari for you (sorry …).

Instead, it will be a person you can get "naked" with—not literally, of course, but someone who gives you a reality check, pushes you forward, and holds you accountable. For me, it's my good friend Jimmy Mills. I can tell him everything that's going on, and he can tell me when I'm being overly sensitive, insecure, or just downright illogical. What's interesting about Jimmy is that he's a 64-year-old retired insurance broker whom you wouldn't necessarily pair with me if you put it all on paper. But find your person. They should be able to

- Tell you uncomfortable truths
- Help you discover hidden talents
- Make potential connections for you

Partner Up

Building a support group also allows you to find a friend who can accompany you when you do have to (or want to) attend a networking event. As Jordana Valencia writes in the *Harvard Business Review*:[8]

"There will be times when you'll have to network more than you want. During these times, consider bringing a coworker with you to help you achieve your networking goals ... bring a friend who is knowledgeable about your business (you can even prepare them beforehand with a company and networking FAQ).

"Bringing a partner with you serves three purposes. First, social support can help reduce exhaustion and burnout, especially if support comes in the form of a tangible service such as networking. Second, you and your partner can divide and conquer. This means

---

8   Jordana Valencia, "How to Keep Networking from Draining You," *Harvard Business Review*, May 9, 2018, https://hbr.org/2018/05/how-to-keep-networking-from-draining-you.

that you can expend less energy and talk to fewer people, but still gather a large number of contacts at the end of the night, thanks to your partner's efforts. To make this strategy even more effective, consider choosing a partner who is more extroverted than you or is naturally energized by social gatherings. That way they're intrinsically motivated and excited to socialize with others."

This can also be an amazing strategy if you're an introvert—go find yourself an extroverted partner to do the hard work for you.

Your Inner Circle

As I mentioned earlier, my support network includes the Great Eight—a group of guys in Atlanta brought together by our common ruthless pursuit of passions who act as my inner circle of my most trusted advisers.

Initially, a few of us were inspired to come together by being part of a formal mastermind group or seeing the success of others who were in a mastermind. There was something really compelling about that, but we didn't want to join someone else's mastermind. We wanted to create our own. So we did.

"I have two rules for friendship. Do my friends make me happy or do they make me better? The men of the Great Eight do both. Not a meet-up goes by either individually or as a group that I don't leave better than I arrived. As an added benefit, I usually laugh until my belly hurts when I'm with these legendary gentlemen. This group has helped and inspired me to be a better leader, husband, and man, and I am eternally grateful for them." —**Tommy Breedlove**

Joining a mastermind is a great way to find supporters. You can really leverage the practicality and input from others. We just happen to have several guys who are very private. Joining a more public mastermind wasn't really in the cards for them, so we just created our own.

Also, when I first began my journey as an author, it took me down this line of helping men to become better men. After hitting a few rock bottoms in my own life, I felt inspired to bring more people together (thanks to the impact that Tommy Breedlove had on my life and the Great Eight). We meet on a monthly basis and help each other become better fathers, better husbands, and better businesspeople.

"Being a part of the Great Eight has held me accountable in relationships, helped me focus on quality time with my parents that wasn't happening, created an aggressive vision for myself and company, celebrated my wins, and asked tough questions in my struggles ... but most importantly, has created a pure environment with no angle or agenda that everyone can be themselves (especially now) and truly wants to help each other grow!" —**Hank McLarty**

Now I look around the table of the Great Eight, and everyone is creating so much of what follows the model I'm trying to inspire with this book, beginning with developing your passion while you continue to use your existing currency. One of our members is a well-known radio host, and he felt uninspired. When we were sitting down together before our holiday dinner last year, he said, "Man, you guys are crushing it! I just need to be challenged."

So I broke it down to his currency: "You get people to listen to you and you change lives that way. And you can do it better than almost anyone out there. You can teach others to use their voice to create better audio content." That was the seed of what has become a podcast consultancy as well as a larger movement and platform, including a book.

Bert Weiss' currency is being one of the top audio talents in the U.S., which naturally led to him developing a business based on his passion of creating a podcast consultancy. He's also turned his radio show into a podcast—one of the top 50 on Apple. Bert has also diversified his ad revenue to digital, which is now in the seven figures with more than six million downloads a month! As I tell everyone I try to inspire in almost any conversation, *this stuff works!* Know your currency and let that give action toward a passion that either compliments a currency you're passionate about (in Bert's case) or encourages you to create something brand new that's more in line with your passions and purpose!

How to Create Your Own Great Eight ... or Fabulous Four ... or Even Terrific Two ...

If you don't know of people in your personal network who might want to form a mastermind with you, hit the internet. Yep, the internet. There are communities for *everything*. With almost any niche, you can find a community, and within each one of those communities, you can use the search parameters in place to find a mastermind, a small group, or a network that you can pay to join to take your stuff to the next level.

It's important that you pay for it because it makes sure you have accountability on your end and that you're valuing the experience. After three months, you can revisit to make sure it's still the right group for you.

These support groups are a really good way of looking at your expertise and your currency, then your passions that you're pursuing, and then the things that you're just beginning. Maybe you want to get into public speaking. It could be learning a new language. You could be donating your time to some nonprofit. But the important thing is that when you talk about what you're pursuing, the other people in your support group challenge you. They might say, "Oh my gosh, yeah, I get paid $20,000, $30,000 for speeches. Let me help you with that. I've got a really good formula for you to follow for some of your speeches" or "I challenge you to do one podcast every week." Or they might give you a punch in the face saying, "That's great, but you're not a good public speaker, so that might not be something that you want to pursue."

There has to be both vulnerability as well as honesty when using the group as a sounding board. This will give you the confidence and credibility to take it to the next level.

By being part of such a group, you can benefit not only from their expertise and experiences but also from their practicality and accountability. Many people talk about big dreams but fail to pursue them or give up after just a few weeks. Find your group and find your accountability for audacious goals.

If you are looking for a place to start, check out my friend Tommy Breedlove's Legendary Life Mastermind. Tommy wrote the Wall Street Journal and USA Today Best Selling book *Legendary: A Simple Playbook for Building and Living a Legendary Life, and Being Remembered as a Legend*. He's also one of my best friends and life-changing mentors. Tommy built a mastermind group called the Legendary Life Mastermind based on his book and coaching. I now have the honor of guest speaking at all of his Legendary Life retreats and mastermind events and have met many people featured in this book by participating in masterminds with Tommy.

Super-Connecting: One of the Most Valuable Currencies (Even with a Small Network)

Recently, I was speaking at a Young President's Organization, or YPO, event and was chatting with the NFL player Larry Fitzgerald in between sessions. He reminded me of a key point: When someone asks you for an introduction, your reputation is on the line. If you introduce a bad seed to a good contact, then your reputation is collateral damage. Do not be tempted to fulfill needs if you don't fully trust and believe in that connection!

As your network grows, your ability to match currencies with needs becomes greater. But that doesn't mean you can't be known (and valued) as a super-connector, even with a small network. Of course, not all connections are equal. If you get careless about who you refer people to, it'll tarnish your reputation. But your willingness to do some legwork to build connections will make others want to be around you. And as you grow your network, you'll be able to make more and better connections.

What does it look like to be a super-connector? Let's look into the mind of a couple of them.

Inside the Mind of a Super-Connector

Dan Scalia is a super-connector. You can tell from the second you meet him. The way his mind works. The way he acts. He's just *always* looking for ways to make mutually beneficial connections for people.

"When I see people who aren't putting as much time, energy, and effort into developing those solid relationships, it reflects poorly on them. I don't lose sight of that. You see over time. There are plenty of people who will reach out to me who just need assistance. But they never lost where I was; they consistently made an effort to check in, catch up. Maybe there's something to work on together. Maybe there *isn't* something to work on together. There's a vested interest in seeing someone's personal growth and career growth happen."

Or take Paul Brown, the CEO of Inspire Brands, which has more than 30,000 restaurants with brands such as Arby's, Dunkin' Donuts, and Jimmy John's. Everyone is trying to get time with or has an ask for Paul. When we sat down to talk about business relationships, he said: "Do you know how many people come into a meeting with a transaction-based mentality? Do you know how many of them have succeeded in doing business with me? I can count on less than one hand. When people develop relationships with me, it's then that we end up doing business together. *Business is a byproduct of connection.*"

Support Networks Help Create Super-Connectors

You need both support networks and super-connectors. Super-connectors are the ones you go to once you're ready. Once you've practiced your currency enough, that's when you start bringing your super-connectors into your networking outreach. You can also use your passions to create this connection.

The most important thing with super-connectors, as Quincy Jones says, is you've always got to keep them warm. You've always got to be bringing value and going in with gives instead of trying to always go for some sort of ask. When you do this, eventually, the ask comes naturally. Many times, the other person will ask *you* how they can help and you never even have to go in for an ask yourself. *Save Your Asks* is an apt title for this book because you need to be constantly honing those relationships.

You also have to show your vulnerability with super-connectors. Trust me, it will bring the facades down. Find something you have in common—say, having daughters—and share your story. "I hear you've raised two amazing daughters," you say. "As the father of girls who are nine and 11, I'd love to know how you got them to stop fighting with one another." Super-connectors become conditioned to being asked for *things*. Finding things you have in common with them will help you deepen the relationship without becoming a taker.

You're going to find that a lot of facades come down. You can then start asking super-connectors for specific advice around your currency, which will lead to much more success than generic (and extremely annoying) questions such as "How do you get ahead in the business world?" or "Can we talk about my new career ideas?" It's absolutely critical that you be as specific as possible. For example: "Do you know anyone who specializes in sports marketing with professional athletes? I have a new brand that I'm building that would be perfect for an endorsement from an MLB pitcher."

"I've found it's not so much vulnerability as it is accessibility. If you can be accessible, it's a good thing." —**Sean Reardon**

Relationships with super-connectors should be treated just like friendships. Find out what interests them, listen actively, and be ready to give, not take. You'd be surprised what talents you bring to the table, whether it's digital savviness or emotional intelligence. As Lydia Fenet (head auctioneer at Christie's and author) so wisely says, "We are *all* just humans trying to do the best we can."

How to Find Super-Connectors

Steer clear of the self-professed "super-connectors" who label themselves as such in their LinkedIn and other social media accounts (if you've done this yourself, remove it immediately). Instead, focus on seeking people out who are at the nexus of your passions and your target. Once you've found them, it's time to use new tactics. Research and ask friends, "Who's the one person I have to meet in order to achieve my dream of [your goal]?" You'll be surprised at how quickly things come together.

There are plenty of ways to establish connections and to push yourself to get outside of your immediate network. It's completely fine to start with social media, which can serve as a tool to slowly build a relationship with that person, whether it be on Instagram, LinkedIn, or Twitter, and develop a genuine connection so someone might open themselves up to a phone call or Zoom.

I've found Instagram to be incredibly effective at building relationships. It's one of the few platforms where you can message super-connectors directly. But make sure you understand what it is that drives them and what types of things they're interested in, which you can learn from their Instagram stories and feed. Also make sure you follow them, comment occasionally on their posts, and then go in for the message. It might take 15 to 20 lightweight interactions before you can ultimately break through, but I promise you, this works! Note to boomers reading: Just *try* it! I promise you'll be surprised at how little a time investment can equate to larger payoffs. It might seem easier to start on LinkedIn, but Instagram gives you easier access to the "untouchables" because you don't have to connect to them first in order to interact with them.

Instagram is also a good way to *deepen* a relationship. For example, I interviewed Alexandra Wilkis Wilson for this book, but most of our back and forth has been on Instagram. Now anytime we hop on a video call, it's like we haven't missed a beat. To reiterate Quincy Jones' point, it's keeping the relationship going that is key. There is no better way to do this with super-connectors than social media.

TL;DR

Stop putting yourself under so much pressure to do everything yourself. Instead, find your crew to help you get to the next level.

Make the Connection

- Start with just one person for your support network.
- Find your extroverted partner for social gatherings (especially if you're an introvert).
- Join or create a group whose members can provide expertise, experiences, a practical voice, and accountability.
- Develop your inner circle and double down on them.
- Remember that the connection economy is one of prosperity, collaboration, and infinite possibilities.

CHAPTER 5:

People to Avoid

Imagine you've decided to train for your first marathon. You've dreamed of running a marathon for years and decided to take the first step to achieving your dream. You're excited to get started and immediately tell three people about your dream.

The first gets very excited for you and asks how she can help. The second congratulates you but then asks whether this is "another one of your one-week wonder" endeavors. The third, a coworker with whom you eat lunch every day, tells you that running is bad for your knees, and that all the things it takes to complete a marathon aren't worth it because it makes you miserable.

Are you more or less likely to train for the marathon after these three conversations? At the end of the first, you're probably more likely. After the second, you might start questioning whether this *is* just another dream you won't follow through with. After the third, you might be discouraged and question whether it's even worth it.

Let's assume you push through anyhow. You download a training and nutrition plan and start right away. You head to the grocery store and meal prep for the first week. You go for your first run the following morning. You show up to work and your coworker scoffs that you brought your own lunch. He asks whether you're going to stop eating lunch with him "now that you're a marathon runner" and acts as if you're abandoning him.

Nevertheless, you persist. You have big goals and you're more motivated than ever. Day after day, you experience the same routine. One person encourages you. Another person acts surprised that you've stuck with it as long as you have. A third person acts as if you're a bad person, even if you still eat lunch with them but just bring your own meals.

How much easier and more enjoyable would your life be if all three of them supported you? Or what if one or two of them connected you with a friend of theirs who has run several marathons to give you a few pointers?

The answer is simple. You'd be much more likely to achieve big things if you spent more time with supporters and super-connectors and less time with people making your goals harder for you.

So who do you need to avoid? The short answer is people who make your goals harder to achieve. They drain your energy. They discourage you no matter what you want to do. They pull you down and convince you that you can't achieve your goals.

When you're aiming big, you need all the help you can get. You can't afford to be running with a weight on your back when you're looking to do something bigger than you've ever done before—especially when you want to build real, sustainable success by saving your asks, developing your networking currencies, and even evolving your currencies to find the place where your passion, purpose, and profession collide.

For the rest of the chapter, I'm going to talk briefly about specific types of people to avoid. Then I'll share some tips about *how* to avoid them because that's often the biggest challenge—especially when some of these people are close friends or even family. (And don't worry, I know that not everyone will be able to completely avoid family, even if they are standing in the way of your achieving your goals. I'll share some tips to help in those circumstances too.)

Here are the most important people to avoid.

Askholes

If you've read this far, it probably comes as no surprise to learn that the first people you need to avoid are askholes. Askholes are unique in the networking world. They're like the Dementors from *Harry Potter* that suck out all the good energy from all around you, and you can feel the impact almost immediately. They go in for ask after ask after ask, almost never offering any "give." They just take, take, take, take, and take some more. They create a sense of dread whenever you see them come up on your caller ID but, for some reason, you feel obliged to answer every tenth or fifteenth call.

When you do enter a conversation with them, they talk only about what they need and forget to ask you, "Hey, so how are you doing?" If they do, they often interrupt you before you've even answered to get back to talking about them and what *they* need.

They ask for introductions to your most precious and valuable connections, often well before they're even ready for that type of connection. And when they do, they're the type of person you *dread* connecting with anyone but another askhole because you don't want them to pester people like they pester you. Not only would it drain the energy of your connection but it would make you look bad by association.

I've developed a very high sensitivity for askholes. To me, an askhole is anyone who goes in for more than two asks back-to-back before offering a helpful connection in return. There are very few exceptions.

"People go wrong when they create a negative association to their identity," says Karissa Kouchis, a corporate trainer for Tony Robbins. "If they go in for the ask too early, or they ask the wrong thing and they do it in the wrong way, every time their name pops up, it's a negative trigger. Maybe they've asked an annoying question, or they've reached out multiple times, or it was the wrong timing. They just don't have the sensory acuity to know good timing." These are usually the same people who have what Karissa calls "LAE," or low-a** energy. You need to bring your "HAE" with passion and purpose instead.

Sure, we have seasons during which we're taking more than giving, but askholes spend their entire lives in the season of taking, and they're taking more than our time; they're taking away our focus on genuine connection as well as just using us for referrals (thereby wasting an ask for you).

I like to approach askholes and use transparency in giving very direct feedback. Call the askhole out. If they continue, this may be controversial, but you just silence them with silence. This is also known as "ghosting" and ghosting hurts. A lot. But don't pick up the phone or text them back. Askholes are very quickly chipping away at your energy because they're not offering anything else. They're just draining you, so nip it in the bud by not responding or just saying "no" to all their requests. You'll be surprised how they eventually stop asking you for stuff just by saying "no" over and over again. If they don't, just ghost. Completely ghost. They're taking you away from your best impact on the world (sorry, but I'm not sorry for anyone reading this who I may have ghosted).

Empty Askers

Here's an example from my own experience with the empty ask that has happened many times in various forms. This example is a bit of a combination of a few of the worst examples to protect the guilty.

I enter a conversation with a new contact, and we get to talking about grilling and grills in our race to the middle (See "The New Networking Terminology" section up front if you need a refresher.)

As a way to connect with this person, I mention I love the Big Green Egg and became almost addicted to buying their products after making a connection at the company who gets me 20 percent off anything they carry. We finish our conversation and move on. He seemed like a good guy, and I was looking forward to getting to know him.

Two weeks later, my phone rings. It's my new contact. First words out of his mouth, "Hey, I really enjoyed meeting you. I'd love to get together again."

I respond: "Sounds great. What did you have in mind?"

Here comes the empty ask.

"You've convinced me. I need to get a Big Green Egg. So I figured we could take a ride down there and continue our conversation. I'll pick up a grill, and we'll get to know each other some more. What do you think? And can you drive since you know where you're going?"

Excuse me?! This dude wants me to drive 45 minutes to get him a grill?!

You have to be very discerning about whom you want to do favors for, but then also make sure that you create boundaries for yourself, especially if you tend to be a people pleaser (like I am). If you're a people pleaser, you *need to* keep aware of your tendencies. Watch out for the empty ask and feel empowered to deny it. If someone asks to tag along with you and someone they've been dying to meet but to whom you don't feel ready to make a connection, just say so. "I'd love to, but she's very protective and private, so I don't violate her trust in me by inviting people to come along" is a perfectly appropriate response. It's also important that you yourself do not become an empty asker. When people offer up something early in a relationship, be discerning of not taking advantage of them with whatever it is they've offered.

Net Energy Takers

When it comes to people in our network, we have to establish a clear line between the givers and the takers. The givers are the people who give us energy—not necessarily connections or things, but just plain energy. They're the ones we actually get excited to see on our caller ID.

Takers are the opposite (oh no … it's Carl calling again … I don't want to answer this). Get rid of the takers in both your network and your life and just focus on the givers. And there are plenty of them. If you find that you get rid of all your takers in your network and you have no givers, then it's time to go back to the drawing board and create a network of givers.

A coach and friend of mine, Tommy Breedlove, couldn't take it anymore. Ben, an associate of his, had been machine-gunning Tommy with ask after ask after ask. So Tommy left Ben this killer voice mail:

> "I'm about to give you the biggest piece of advice that anybody's ever going to give you in your entire life. I'm going to tell you how I manage my inbox, my text box, all the social media messages: I watch out for net takers.

And Ben, my brother, *you are a net taker*. Every time you've called me for the past year and a half, you've wanted something from me. You never ask how I'm doing. You never ask how my practice is. You've never offered to give me anything in return. All you do is take, take, take ... My friend Chris Tuff calls it an askhole. And so this is the biggest advice I can give you. First thing is, if people are taking from you and your network, your inbox, your voice mail, and they just constantly want something, just start ignoring them and they'll go away. Second thing is, don't be an askhole. Be a net giver, not a taker. And trust me, brother, your network is loaded with net takers. So they have trained you well. So, brother, I'm being very serious here. You've called me 50 times over the last two years. Every single time you've wanted something, and you've never offered me anything in return. That's the biggest advice I can give you. Be a giver. Change it now and you'll be even more successful. I love you, man. Hope the best for you, but you can't keep taking from your brother. See ya."

Net takers are usually the same people who are emotional vampires and askholes. Mark Manson, author of *The Subtle Art of Not Giving a F*ck*, among other books, does a great job identifying these:

- An excessive need for validation or attention from others—the conversation is always about them and their needs.
- The belief that little to nothing that occurs is their fault—they will constantly play the victim card and blame others.
- The lack of self-awareness to recognize their self-defeating patterns.

Net takers drain your brain of energy. When you get back from hanging out with them or get off the phone with them, the last thing you want to do is continue to work. You just feel like taking a nap. And, many times, that's exactly what you do. Another day wasted because a net taker drained you of your energy.

"Yeah But-ers"

Yeah but-ers are *everywhere*. These are the persistently negative people, the devil's advocates, who will tell you *every* reason why your dream won't come true. They'll come up with every reason possible, throw out every cliché in the book like "It takes money to make money" or "It's not what you know but who you know" to make you think the deck is stacked against you.

The truth is the yeah but-ers are often more afraid for and self-conscious about themselves than they are concerned about you. Some have given up on their dreams and want to feel better about themselves by not watching as you and others achieve your dreams. Others believe *they* don't have what it takes to achieve their dreams, so they tell you "It takes money to make money" or some other bogus cliché to keep you from proving them wrong.

The best thing you can do with the yeah but-ers is to keep pushing forward and lead by example. They *need* to see someone just like them achieve more to convince them it's possible for them too. Be the example. Keep pushing. Be encouraging. But do it from a bit of a distance because they can be convincing.

The Best Way to Avoid These People

By far, the best way to avoid these people is to do it *before* they infiltrate your network. It's not always possible, of course. Some of these people share homes (or beds) with us. We'll talk about those people in a bit. But many of these people are future connections—people you'll meet in the future. Filter them out before they get in.

No matter how experienced you become, your filter will be imprecise. It'll get better over time, but it'll never be perfect. You're going to have to differentiate between the self-proclaimed super-connectors and the ones who actually do it. You'll also have to differentiate between transactional supporters and super-connectors and the true ones who do it because they genuinely want to do good in the world and for the people they are connecting. It's about understanding intention.

I have an admittedly imprecise formula I put people through as I look to bring them into my trust network. Here's how it works.

I talk with them for a while to sense what they emphasize. If they emphasize their own success, it gives me pause. If they emphasize how they helped other people become successful, it tells me they enjoy helping others. As I learn the person's intentions, I then weigh that with what I see about their ego and level of influence and connections. If they seem to care more about their own success than helping others, have a big ego, and have few high-quality connections, they get a red light (no go). If they have mostly positive qualities in those areas, they get a green light (go for it). If it's a mostly mixed bag, they get a yellow light, which means they're on pause. This allows me to let in the people who are genuine and authentic and who want to truly do good in the world. Note, some people will actually float in what I call "purgatory" or a yellow light until I can adequately get enough qualitative data to put them in red or green.

When someone gets a red light, I'll give them a second shot to make sure my filter wasn't off. If the second shot confirms my suspicions, I'll tell them I don't think I can help them but wish them well. I'll be cordial if they initiate an email but won't initiate conversation. I respect their time and mine more than to force a connection that's not a good fit. If that sounds tough, it can be. But the alternative is worse. The alternative is both of you wasting each other's time.

How to Avoid These People After They Infiltrate Your Network

Let's get one truth out in the open here: Everybody has at least one friend or family member who would never make the cut if they weren't related or a long-term friend. Every successful person. Every CEO. Every entrepreneur. Everyone. I have yet to meet a single person who didn't have at least one askhole, empty asker, net energy taker, or yeah but-er in their close friend or family network.

That means you *can* be successful even if one or more of these people have infiltrated your most sacred inner circle. How? The solution requires three steps.

First, don't let any more of them in. These people can *drain* you. Limit the damage by only allowing genuine supporters and super-connectors in.

Second, set strong boundaries. You're not going to change their ways with words, but you can change their ways by leading by example over a *long* period of time. As the old saying goes, the people who called you crazy when you started will eventually ask you how you did it. It won't happen every time, but it happens a lot. If an askhole cousin of yours keeps asking for favors, it's perfectly fine to say that you won't be making connections for them. If they keep asking, set that boundary where you tell them you just want to keep your relationship personal and encourage them to build their own network. If a yeah but-er friend tells you all the reasons you won't be able to achieve your goal, tell them you're building a network of people who have done it before and prefer to keep your relationship with them separate from your business.

Third, get busy with supporters and super-connectors. Sometimes, the best defense is a good offense. You might not be able to avoid your brother-in-law who spends the entire time complaining about how half the world is out to get him and the other half owes him something completely. But that doesn't mean you have to go golfing with him every week. Schedule time with more positive influences. Fill up your calendar with positive influences and cut down the time with your closer negative influences to the bare essentials.

TL;DR

You're wasting your time and energy with the wrong networks. Get rid of the askholes in your life and jam forward with people you truly connect with.

Make the Connection

- Make a list of the positive, encouraging people in your life who add energy to you—focus on those relationships.
- Make a mental note of the askholes, empty askers, net energy takers, and yeah but-ers in your life and start getting rid of them.
- Start scheduling time to talk with the positive, supportive people on your first list so you don't have as much time to spend with the people who pull you down. Seriously, do it right now. Send at least three of them a text or message asking to get together next week.

CHAPTER 6:

You and Your Brand

You have a plan. You have some people and know the type of people you want more of in your life. Now you need a brand. Don't worry, building a memorable brand is pretty easy. You don't need to hire a big ad agency like mine or even a solo branding expert to come up with some elaborate plan to make you a household name. You just need to identify something about you that you enjoy and that others will remember. For me, it's as simple as a color. Yes, a color.

Like 164 million other American adults, I wear glasses. But unlike 163,999,999 of them, I don't wear just *any* glasses; I wear a pair of custom frames made in Nike Volt Yellow (I have four different styles in this shade). The super bright color struck me when I was buying an Apple Watch Nike series, and now it splashes across everything from my specs to my pens to my shoes and even my car. The rims, handles, mirrors, and brakes are all Nike Volt Yellow. You'll read more of this story in a bit, but now I'm the guy with neon yellow accessories. It's become how people recognize me—my brand, if you will.

Not a day goes by when someone doesn't comment on my car, sneakers, notebook, or glasses. Actually, out of all the questions I've received in interviews or speeches, the most common one is, "Where did you get those glasses?!" I'm quick to answer that they're from an awesome little shop in Atlanta called Ansley Eye Care. The same is true when I'm at a concert or traveling through Hartsfield (the busiest airport in the world) as people recognize the Volt Yellow and yell, "Yo, Tuff!"

More importantly, my personal brand has led directly to hundreds of connections and dozens of deep relationships. Yes, I now do a bunch of work with Nike, and it's not unusual for a pair of sneakers in Volt Yellow to show up at my door. But I wear the color less to impress and more to make connections with potential clients, customers, and friends. It's a conversation opener. And it makes me *memorable*. As Lydia Fenet points out, it's essential that we differentiate ourselves from others with stories as well as with our own branding—the stories follow our appearances!

The other place I double down on my brand is the tattoo art on my arms and legs. Every part of each of my tattoos tells a story about my journey, and you'll see samples of it sprinkled throughout the book and my cover. These are all a product of my close friend Keoki from Perpetual Roots. I've spent more than 35 hours in his chair, and we now have a deep and genuine connection for life. I can simply engage in a conversation with Keoki who will then freehand a perfect interpretation of my intentions. His tattoos are now about to be applied to a new SUV I bought, and they can be found on the cover of this book!

One of my favorite memories is appearing live on *The Bert Show* as Keoki tattooed my right-arm half-sleeve with images of bringing the world together through connection. It was a win-win-win for personal branding. My friend Bert Weiss was able to entertain his listeners by interviewing me as I endured the pain of getting tattooed. Keoki got his name out there as a tattoo artist. And my first book, *The Millennial Whisperer*, got even more publicity. In fact, I got a speaking engagement at a multibillion-dollar company because the coordinator heard me on *The Bert Show*. People remember stories—figure out what story you're telling *before* you arrive at that dinner table!

And I'm only one of countless other people who have learned to establish their personal brand. Your personal brand is on par with your support network and your super-connectors, and it allows you to achieve the confidence and mindset for success, which we'll discuss in the next chapter. For now, we're going to dive into the dynamic world of personal branding, how it represents you, and how not to become branded a networking askhole.

Decide what you want to become and then make decisions and take actions that lead you in the direction of that future.

The "Google Me" Exercise

Imagine your life three years from now. You want people to find you through Google. What search terms would they use? These terms should determine your passions because they suggest topics about which you are passionate.

For example, my friend Meghan is currently a software developer, but she's passionate about fabric art. She wants to open her own gallery of fabric art in three years. When people are looking to browse or buy fabric art, they'd google "fabric art gallery" or "fabric artist," and, ideally, discover Meghan. Fabric art is her passion.

Once you've done the Google Me exercise, you can keep working this muscle by designing exercises around your passions. In Meghan's case, this might be reaching out to a well-known fabric artist once a month for coffee or building the connection with a person who has the perfect spot to lease for her gallery.

My Google Me terms would be kitesurfing, travel, being the father of young girls, Big Green Eggs, and even helping identify and trade people's currencies! It's these search terms that will help guide your passions.

The 3 Cs of Connection

If you were to ask me the fastest way of evolving from "networking" to "connecting," I'd tell you about the power of 3 Cs: currency, curiosity, and confidence.

Currency: Understand what you hold in terms of your currency inside of conversations. Use this currency to create the connection. If you're an advertiser, talk about your advertising. If you're a writer, talk about your writing. Make sure that after your conversation that person can walk away knowing that if they need something relating to your expertise, they can talk to you.

Curiosity: Express genuine curiosity about the person you are trying to connect with. Ask questions and find that middle ground (a race to the middle), and don't be afraid to get deeper in the conversation instead of staying at a high level.

Confidence: You must exhibit confidence when connecting with others. This is more of a learned skill than anything else and might take more repetition. Practice this with every interaction.

If you consistently work on the 3 Cs of Connection, you will build a strong reputation as someone others want to connect with—and make connections for.

Fortunately, developing the 3 Cs of Connection is a natural byproduct when you aim big, understand and feel passionate about your currencies, and focus on building authentic relationships with supporters and super-connectors.

What Have You Become?

As I'm finishing up writing this book, I'm raving to my network about *In and Of Itself*, the film based on the nearly 600 performances that comedian, magic consultant, and all-around amazing Derek DelGaudio delivered at New York City's Daryl Roth Theatre. Directed by the man behind the Muppets (Frank Oz) and produced by Neil Patrick Harris, *In and Of Itself* is described as a modern allegory. For me, it's a reflection of identity and a way to reframe how we think of ourselves as we operate in the new world of networking. I'll refrain from getting into too many details because you know what I mean if you've seen the movie. If you haven't, go find it online; it's worth every penny for a streaming service and every minute of your time.

Derek opens his show with this rumination:

"They ask you, 'What do you want to be when you grow up?'

"… Later they ask you, 'What do you do?'

"Which is just another way of saying, 'What have you become?'

"So you search, you look at the roles the world offers you, trying to find the one that reflects you."

Whoa. I could instantly envision the hundreds of people I've consulted with navigating these very questions. As Derek goes on to explore through some pretty fantastic feats, our identities are so much more of a kaleidoscope than a mirror. The audience is asked upon entry to the Daryl Roth Theatre to select an "I Am" card that reflects who they are: a ninja, a single mother, an adventurer, a visionary. By the end of the show, nearly everyone (including Derek) is in tears, and probably you will be too as he metaphorically flips the cards around.

You might be stocking the shelves at Publix right now, professionally, but you are also a father, a son, a baseball player, and a public servant. I might be an advertising executive, but I'm also an author, a friend, a husband, and the guy in the Nike Volt Yellow glasses. We're all shifting in and out of these currents, finding out which one will carry us along to fulfillment.

That person you're trying to connect with for the next phase of your career, a new job, or a chance to surf for a living? She's an entrepreneur and CEO—and a runner, an aunt, a dancer, and a part-time barista with a penchant for making mocha lattes spiked with cayenne pepper.

Says Derek, "I remember reading that true identity, and not just identity, is that which exists within one's own heart and is seen by another."

Steps to Transition Your Currency

1. Focus on Your Existing Currency
   a. Don't ditch your existing currency
   b. Focus on constantly improving your existing currency
2. Cultivate New Currency
   a. Focus a small part of your efforts on cultivating your passion into another currency
   b. Use your existing currency to fund and build connections relating to your new passion
3. Scale Connections Using Your New Passion
   a. Focus more time and attention on using your new currency to build connections
4. Scale Out of Your Old Currency
   a. When you spend most of your time networking using a currency of your own choosing, and one about which you're passionate, work no longer feels like work.

Go Bananas

Speaking of yellow, have you ever tried to buy a ticket to see the Coastal Plain League's Savannah Bananas baseball team play? If you haven't, good luck. Season after season, the team has sold out every seat in the house—a feat many thought impossible just a few short years before Jesse Cole came to town.

When Jesse decided to bring another baseball team to Savannah, Georgia, he was nearly laughed out of the city. Team after team had tried to make it work at Grayson Stadium for 90 years. Many people thought the stadium was the problem, even leaving the city because they could not get public funding to build a new stadium.

Even with billions of dollars being spent promoting baseball throughout the country, the new generation of sports fans was turning elsewhere than baseball for their fix. It wasn't until Cole decided to add his own personal brand—wearing a bright yellow tuxedo—among other things to the Savannah Bananas that the stadium that others thought could never field a successful team saw success.

Unlike the results of his predecessors, the Savannah Bananas saw immediate success both on and off the field. In fact, when they launched the team on February 25, 2015, they immediately received national recognition: trending on Twitter and receiving shout-outs on *SportsCenter* and *Good Morning America* within 24 hours. They sold merchandise to all 50 states and 6 countries. In their very first season, they sold out 18 of 25 games, broke the stadium attendance record, and won the Coastal Plain League Championship.

How? It all started with branding.

"Here's something I've learned in my 10-plus years in the entertainment industry," writes Cole in *Find Your Yellow Tux: How to Be Successful by Standing Out*. "Forget the business you're in. Forget your industry. Forget your market. Forget your location. If you can find your yellow tux, you can find success. What is your yellow tux? It's the one thing that makes you and your business stand out—the best version of your*self*."

Cole and the Bananas created a memorable brand and an even more memorable in-stadium experience for their fans. And it immediately translated into more people wanting to be associated with them, both on and off the field.

Jesse loves his yellow tux and fun, quirky branding for the Bananas. It fits who he is and the people he wants to attract.

Your Brand Story

While Jesse Cole's signature color is yellow and mine is Nike Volt Yellow, Rory Cooper's is purple—as in Purple Strategies, a management reputation firm in Washington, D.C., whose clients include McDonald's and BP, among others.

When he sees people struggling to find long-lasting and meaningful connections, Rory has observed that it's often because they're not bold enough to show their true colors. For example, "People who want to be thought leaders feel like they need to comment on everything," he says. "But the problem is that when you're commenting on everything, you're devaluing your opinion, and people will discount your level of expertise."

As I was writing this book, Rory was working with education officials to help decide whether K–12 schools should be open during the coronavirus pandemic. While he doesn't have a master's in education, he spent enough time researching the subject to develop a level of expertise which, combined with his 22-plus years of working with the government, made him a go-to person for conversations on potential K–12 openings. And what makes Rory so in-demand is how he built his personal brand: "I'm really Rory Cooper, the political strategist who has opinions on multiple fronts," he says.

The "purple" reference in Rory's business name reflects the color you get when you combine red and blue. For those who are not as into politics as Rory, red (Republican) and blue (Democrat) are the colors commonly associated with the two main political parties in the U.S. Rory wants to maintain his reputation as the political strategist who understands and respects where everyone comes from.

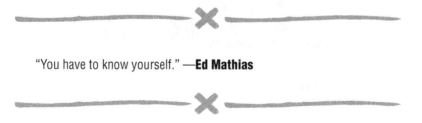

"You have to know yourself." —**Ed Mathias**

When people tweet something negative about him, Rory conveys respect for where they're coming from and also stands by his perspective. When they ask him a question, he does the same.

"A challenge for me has been how to connect that personal brand with Purple." As Rory explains, his name gets about 75 percent of the Google alerts for Purple; he brings the company into the news even without discussing his clients. By building his personal brand the way he has, Rory's been able to create an extraordinary amount of trust regarding government affairs. "I've developed a real personality that exists beyond what I say about politics or what I do for a living," he says. "It gives people a little bit more permission to stick with me through opinions they don't like."

Be Yourself: Authenticity and Confidence

Lydia Fenet, the Global Managing Director of Strategic Partnerships and Lead Benefit Auctioneer at Christie's auction house, is six feet tall. But when she first started raising her gavel, she felt about four feet tall as she masked her true self in order to play the auctioneer part.

"When I started when I was 24 years old, I did not feel comfortable at all," she says. "I actually got on stage with a British accent and put on a black suit like every man I saw. And now that I've been doing auctions and I know what I'm doing and I have full confidence in my abilities, I'm wearing a bright red dress with four-inch heels and huge earrings. I feel comfortable as me."

For Lydia, authenticity and confidence now go hand in hand. "When it comes to sales, when it comes to networking, when it comes to negotiations, the key is feeling confident—confident in yourself, confident in your sales ability, your networking ability," she says. "If you don't feel confident enough, fake it until you do, because that is what we have all done." Lydia has taught me a method she learned with her gavel. When she goes on stage, she slams down the gavel to get the attention of her audience. When she goes into meetings, she mentally imagines striking down the gavel, allowing her to approach that meeting or conversation with the confidence necessary to develop a lasting connection. Now, I imagine laying down my own gavel of confidence as I enter meetings.

When it comes to one-on-one networking—when you are sitting across the table from someone—it's that authenticity that you need to bring to the table, says Lydia. "For me onstage, a lot of times authenticity is about sharing something. I found that whenever I was acting like a British man, no one paid attention." But as she writes in *The Most Powerful Woman in the Room Is You*, a breakthrough came when she was feeling so ill, she couldn't pretend to be anyone—anyone but herself. Instead of rattling off rote details of the lot (a private tour of a board member's art collection), she told a story of how the art collector had once given her relationship advice, and this provided a once-in-a-lifetime experience. "This very small change in selling—inserting something from my own life into that moment—made people stop talking and start to listen," she writes. "In that moment, it clicked. A lightbulb went off. Sell as myself. Sell as me. Why would I bore someone with the details of a lot without creating a story for the person in front of me?"

"Just be your genuine, truest, most authentic self, always paying attention to what is placed in front of you. It's through that *attention* that we begin to see the *intention* of life, and how we are always right where we need to be for the betterment of our personal growth and development." —**Ken Hannaman**

Become a Currency Broker

As I discussed in the preface to this book, I've realized that I can help people barter currencies in a way that benefits both people by connecting them with each other. Although I do so expecting nothing in return, I frequently gain a lot of personal benefit from doing so. I deepen relationships with each of the people, and sometimes they even introduce me to others.

Anyone can be a currency broker. Jenny, one of my favorite coffee-shop managers, has become an elite-level currency broker. Jenny has her master's degree in psychology. She knows people. She loves people. So, while she's steaming milk, pouring a dark roast, or sweeping the floors, she's talking to her customers, listening to their stories. These are people who come in every day like clockwork, so Jenny has really gotten to know them well. But she didn't stop there. She also developed a knack for introducing customers to each other based on needs and common interests and talents. Architects have met new clients looking to build homes. Writers have met other writers. Customers have even married each other after being introduced by Jenny.

The Glasses Are Half Full

What you are wearing, and how you appear, is part of your personal brand; as Lydia shares, it gives you confidence, and it gives you authenticity. But yet we always feel constrained to conform to those around us.

It took years for me to evolve my personal brand through authenticity and confidence. I remember how excited I was to get a pair of Ray-Bans, but I got bored of the brown color. I tried red, which didn't work for me, and then I decided to get white glasses. I had them for four years, and I noticed how they became my brand. So when I discovered Nike Volt Yellow, I knew it could become my brand.

Everything I do revolves around how we can bring more light into the world. What translates that better than Nike Volt Yellow?

When I had my new Audi color-matched, I got more comments. "Every time I see your car, I just smile," people say. It makes my wife embarrassed because she thinks (knows?) it's a little ridiculous (she likes to fly underneath the radar). A bright color might not be for you, and that's okay! Find something different that makes you authentic to who you are at your core. As I tell so many people, it takes confidence to be the puppeteer instead of the puppet. Be a leader and not a follower.

Your Struggle Can Shape Your Brand

Personal brands go much deeper than yellow glasses or tuxedos, of course. Consider Jay and Katherine Wolf, who were going after their careers in L.A. when Katherine had a catastrophic stroke. She had a 16-hour brain surgery, 11 operations in total, and spent 40 days in the ICU plus a year in neurological rehab as a result of her stroke. She is still recovering.

Instead of trying to force themselves back into the lives they'd been living before the stroke, Jay and Katherine chose to turn their experience into Hope Heals, a community for people with disabilities. As they write on the Hope Heals website:

At first glance, our story seems exceptional. Without warning, our lives took a detour so sharp and unexpected that few people should be able to relate. Katherine now lives with disabilities, and we've earned hard won wisdom that seemingly places us in a category of our own. But if we've learned anything in our second-chance life, it's that the most personal stories are actually the most universal.

Who among us feels fully free, even when he can walk on his own? Who feels truly beautiful, even when her face is not paralyzed? Who feels completely understood, even without a speech impairment? The answer is a resounding no one. We are all disabled. Some of our "wheelchairs" are simply on the inside instead of the outside.

If you have a pulse, you have problems and you have pain. But you also have a purpose that is simultaneously good and hard. When we choose to embrace the lives we're living this very day and release the lives we wished for, we can know in our deepest places that this good story is being written by a God who can't write any other kind of story. Living the good/hard life means we no longer need to numb ourselves to the difficult and the dark. We can awaken to the broken-down, miraculous nature of our second-chance lives and begin this very day to live them well to the very end.

Katherine and Jay illuminate the essence of human connection: recognizing the power of choosing to embrace the lives we're living this very day. They provide a great example of taking life by the reins, letting their difficulties inspire them to blossom into even better people.

Katherine had a pretty dire hand dealt to her, and you might not feel like you can relate to that level of high drama. But everyone has gone through trials and tribulations that have played a part in shaping their character. Digging into the unique situations that have altered or defined your journey might be a great place to start looking for a personal brand you can own.

Superhero Super-Connector

When your trainer shows up in a Marvel T-shirt and X-Men socks, you know you've met your kryptonite. That's because this trainer is Tramell Smith, one of Atlanta's top fitness coaches. An All-American track star at the University of Illinois and a professional runner for two years, Tramell has now turned his talents into torturous workouts that push each and every client to the best of their fitness ability.

What's really amazing about Tramell, though, is the personal brand that began during his college days, when a photo of him raising his hands in victory gave birth to a persona named Victor E. Mann. Along came a logo, activewear, and the Instagram handle of @darkskint_clarkkent that all pay homage to his love for Marvel Comics and his passion for unlocking superhuman powers in his clients.

Thanks to this personal branding, Tramell has an electric connection with people and a reputation that earns him referral after referral.

Set It. Love It. Own It.

So what's your brand? The beauty is that you get to decide. And then you get to take ownership of living your brand. Nike Volt Yellow sunglasses? Bright yellow tuxedo? Being the political strategist who respects opinions from both sides of the political aisle? Reinterpreting rehabilitation? You choose, just do *something* that will set you apart.

"Unapologetically stand in the culture and the experiences that made you who you are because that's the most unique thing you have to offer to anybody." —**Kerry Abner**

Once you choose, take a few minutes to start seeing yourself how others might see you as you build your brand. Then *invest in yourself and in building the brand you want to be known for!*

TL;DR

It's time for you to stand out from the crowd, so go ahead and create a unique brand for yourself. People remember stories. What story are people going to share after meeting you?

Make the Connection

- Remember the 3 Cs: currency, curiosity, and confidence.
- Always revisit your currency when networking—this is your foundation.
- Confidence is the backbone of effective networking: practice, practice, practice. Start with your friends and family, and then start scheduling interviews on podcasts.
- Be yourself when developing your brand—have the courage to stand out. Figure out how you're going to do one thing to enhance your *visual* brand (this could be anything from a particular hat or pair of shoes to a purple car or lime-green bicycle).
- Your personal brand allows you to achieve the confidence and mindset for success.
- Voicing your opinions (respectfully) is part of your personal brand.
- Give your personal brand away, even if it's as simple as a smile.

PART 3:

WHERE PASSION, PURPOSE, AND PROFESSION COLLIDE

CHAPTER 7:

Your Head

In 2018, I took a deep breath and signed for the biggest personal loan of my life: $200,000.

I wasn't going to buy a house.

I wasn't going to charter a yacht to impress clients.

I was going to write a book.

When I called my banker (and friend) Philipp about the loan, he asked me, "Chris, *what* are you doing?!"

Like many people, he thought I was crazy. And maybe I was a little bit. But I knew exactly what I was doing; I was going to make an impact by sharing everything I knew about treating people with empathy in *The Millennial Whisperer*.

What did I do with the money? Thanks to advice from my older brother Alex, I hired an expert for everything, starting with the best book strategist I could find, who knows better than anyone how to write an amazing book that's fun to read, *actually* helps readers, and helps lead the author toward their goals. From there, I made sure I had the best editing, formatting, and marketing money could buy. I knew the book would be helpful and wanted to get it in as many hands as possible.

Within two years of *The Millennial Whisperer*'s publication, the impact has been profound. As I write, I've shared the book and its lessons on more than 500 podcasts. My speeches have impacted millions of people around the world—one presentation alone impacted over 15 million employees via their HR professionals tuning in from India, Europe, the Philippines, and beyond. It's currently in airports, bookstores, and libraries all over the world.

I have also built thousands of new connections while deepening those among my close friends and colleagues. Hank McLarty and Bert Weiss, two members of the Great Eight, are now writing books of their own, expanding the ripple effect of *The Millennial Whisperer* with their own messages. I've become an expert at not only writing books but also positioning books for lead generation and building relationships and connections that create future business and return on investment.

When I first started this journey, I had *no* idea what I was doing. If you had googled my name just two and half years ago, the only thing that would show up had to do with social and digital media because that had been my currency. But through this relentless pursuit of my passion and purpose to inspire and connect with younger workers, my currency became my power to connect. Today, aside from one or two links directly to my agency and professional bio, you have to click through several pages of search results to find anything having to do with social and digital media when you search my name.

Why do I share this story? Because the first step to finding the point where passion, purpose, and profession collide is what some people refer to as "headwork." We started a little bit of the headwork when identifying your personal brand. To actually achieve your big vision, you need to essentially reprogram how you think about yourself in the present *and* the future. It also requires you to develop strong mental fortitude, resilience, and tenacity because there *will* be bumps in the road. You *will* struggle. You *will* believe you are in over your head. It happens to all of us.

Here's the headwork you need to push through when times get tough on your way to the wonderful point where your passion, purpose, and profession collide.

Start With a Growth Mindset

Networking, as we've discussed, is all about relationships. Establishing new relationships makes us smarter—and also requires a growth mindset, which Carol Dweck has written about extensively.

"Individuals who believe their talents can be developed (through hard work, good strategies, and input from others) have a growth mindset," writes Dweck in *Harvard Business Review*. "They tend to achieve more than those with a more fixed mindset (those who believe their talents are innate gifts). This is because they worry less about looking smart and they put more energy into learning."[9]

Those of us who invest in relationships also have a growth mindset, as much as our efforts may exclude a good portion of the population. "When we see people with outstanding interpersonal skills, we don't really think of them as gifted," writes Dweck in her book *Mindset: The New Psychology of Success*. "We think of them as cool people or charming people. When we see a great marriage relationship, we don't say these people are brilliant relationship makers. We say they're fine people. Or they have chemistry. Mean-

---

9   Carol Dweck, "What Having a 'Growth Mindset' Actually Means," *Harvard Business Review*, January 13, 2016, https://hbr.org/2016/01/what-having-a-growth-mindset-actually-means.

ing what? Meaning that as a society, we don't understand relationship skills. Yet everything is at stake in people's relationships."

Resilience and Tenacity

Achieving anything big requires you to build a foundation of resilience and tenacity. By definition, you will be doing things you've never done before. That means you need to take action based on the faith that it will lead to results in the future, not from prior experience taking those actions.

For example, take Randy Smith from Heritage Flooring, who I talked about earlier in the book. A lot of Randy's success comes from his resilience and tenacity. "Almost every week for years, I went to all of the largest home builders and brought them donuts," he says. "And it was often years later they would say, 'All right, Randy, we're going to give you a shot.' It was that absolute tenacity and perseverance that got me to where we are today."

As the Global Influence and Social Actions Lead at Beats/Apple, Astor Chambers has also practiced a long-term approach of resilience and tenacity. It began when he was a student at the Fiorello H. LaGuardia High School of Music & Art and Performing Arts—the "Fame" high school from the TV show—where Astor was asked to take a visitor on a tour. "I didn't think anything of it," he says. "But at the end of the day, she said, 'Hey, I would love for you to come by the office to talk about products and shoes.' Turns out, she worked for Nike."

Turns out, she was Betsy Parker, the sister of Nike CEO Mark Parker. She became a friend and a mentor. "This was networking, but I didn't know it at the time," says Astor, "because I was building a relationship."

When Betsy floated the idea of Astor working at Nike, she said he needed sales experience and suggested he work in retail. "So what did I do?" asks Astor. "Every summer in college I worked at Foot Locker." Fast forward a few years and Astor found himself as the tech guru for Nike. He has since become one of the most sought-after experts on the latest and hottest in branding trends. He credits Betsy with maneuvering him in just the right direction, and he has had the resilience and tenacity to stay laser-focused on his currency and other passions while maintaining this important relationship. "I listened and I did the things that this person provided for me, not did for me," he says. "It's totally about the asks, the networking, and the how."

Fighting Your Fears by *Facing* Your Fears

Like many others I interviewed, Bogdan Constantin found confidence in authenticity by facing his fears. He's the founder and CEO of Voxie and managed to raise millions of dollars for the company during the pandemic—while helping struggling businesses communicate and market themselves through the messaging platform. He's also one of the best storytellers I've ever met—just google how he founded Voxie. It's a long way from his childhood seeking asylum from Romania after the Iron Curtain fell, fleeing with his parents, eventually making their way to Atlanta, where they lived in the Section 8 affordable housing section of the city.

"Fundamentally, I get confidence from the fact I've come from the bottom," says Bogdan. "I know what the bottom is, where the bottom is. So what more do I have to fear? What more do I have to be afraid of?"

Bogdan also remains true to himself, recognizing, as many of the great super-connectors do, that we are essentially all one and the same. This is one of the most important parts of building your brand. "How I connect to people comes down to authenticity," says Bogdan, who has no qualms using the words "dude" and "bro" with CEOs. "I will talk how I talk, and I will be how I am.

People are naturally comfortable because they see that I don't have airs or fakeness. I am 100 percent real in every aspect of my life and how I interact with people."

I'm still amazed by how much authenticity makes a positive impact on success. After I gave a speech to the Total Life Freedom Community, run by Vincent Pugliese, most of the positive feedback centered on how relatable I seemed in discussing how to be intentional while making connections with people who seem out of our league. And I know a piece of that authenticity is being bold enough to wear Nike Volt Yellow.

Exercise: Change Your Networking Energy

Try this cool trick from Jasen Trautwein to transition from fear to abundance when you're setting relationship-building goals.

1. Clench your hand into a fist.
2. Turn it over and spread out your palm.
3. Feel the difference in your hand between the two movements. The clenched fist is fear and scarcity. The open palm is abundance.
4. In social settings, your hands may be loose at your sides, but they could really be invisibly clenched in fear and scarcity.
5. Stretch out your palms to remind yourself of abundance. This will remind you to build relationships with a receptive, abundant attitude.

Practice this while you're reading emails, talking with your spouse, or driving (with one hand still on the wheel, please). You'll be amazed at how much deeper you begin to breathe and how much better you begin to feel.

Slow Down to Speed Up

One common myth about networking is that your speed will determine your success. Want to achieve more? Do more. That's the mindset many (bad) networkers have.

But let me ask you something. What do Visa, Harley-Davidson, AOL, and McDonald's have in common?

Well, one thing they all have in common is that they are just a few of the iconic brands Shelley Paxton helped popularize during a super successful 26-year marketing career—which she abruptly walked away from in 2016 when she realized her day job was draining her soul. Shelley became the Chief Soul Officer of her own life and has since been consulting with others on how to do the same and sharing her lessons through her book, *Soulbbattical: A Corporate Rebel's Guide to Finding Your Best Life.*

"What you need to do is carve out time for yourself," says Shelley of the mindset required for leveraging the most out of your life. "And that time for yourself starts with learning to sit still, which is the hardest freaking thing for high achievers to do. We've been conditioned to become human doings over human beings."

Slowing down and refueling can be the best way to get our currencies and passions back on track, says Shelley. "Sometimes refueling is simply doing more of what lights you on fire," she says. "What are you doing that's fueling your energy and, as a result, fueling your life?" Shelley also advocates for making time off from your job a prerequisite for smart work, creativity, and innovation. "When we flip that time-off script, we are choosing to be in service of ourselves, our energy, and our impact in the world," she says. "What do we do with our time to fuel more of our passion, well-being, and impact?"

While Shelley intentionally stepped away from her marketing role to slow down, super-connector Kerry Abner found himself forced into a different pace when he was laid off from his longtime corporate job in 2014. How would he afford rent, gas, and more? The Atlanta-based entrepreneur took the opportunity to reflect and eventually create his own agency, Intecoo, which connects culture and brands for such clients as Sony Music.

"It pushed me to new levels of creativity, resourcefulness, and awareness because I was the source, the sole provider for my life, and I found a rhythm in that eventually the fear stopped," says Kerry. "There are a lot of people with jobs who would completely lose their minds if they got fired because they feel like, without their jobs, they can't do anything. But this is a very unprecedented time during which we have a direct-to-consumer market. And if you have consistency, effort, and clarity in what your offer is to the market that you're serving, this is the best time to try your hand at building something. I didn't take another job until I felt aligned with what I was doing." It's also important to note that Kerry is now raising money for his side hustle called Manhattan Grey, which is a hair care product with the goal "to encourage more black men and women to embrace their grey hair in confidence and stop using harmful dye and chemicals." (He's already done over $75K in sales!)

We must consistently revisit our own passions and purpose because we change with age and experiences, but our jobs and currency fail to keep up with that. We will be more successful in our jobs, better connected, and more fulfilled if we slow down to speed up. Remember SMARTEST goals—is this goal seasonally appropriate?

Do you need to slow down in order to speed up?

Have Fun

When you go from earning a law degree at Oxford University and working with the Obama administration to growing a chia seed business, you learn a thing or two about the possibilities available when you pursue your passions. That's the evolution Shane Emmett made.

Shane's the cofounder of Health Warrior, which sells chia seed bars, among other products, and has been acquired by PepsiCo. (Fun fact: his supplier had a minimum order of 25,000 pounds for chia seeds, a fact Shane's roommates learned the hard way when their apartment quickly became a chia seed storage facility.)

"The best way to start side hustles is as a hobby, where you're having fun with it," says Shane. "And then the initial market is your friends and family. Word of mouth will tell you whether you should spend money on it or not." Shane recalls sharing an email address with his cofounders. "We just emailed ourselves internally, which doesn't make any sense," he says with a laugh. "Some of these emails, you can just see how unbelievably clueless we were, but how much fun we were having with it at the same time." For 18 months, Shane and his cofounders crafted and shared their story, which Shane paraphrases as: "We were athletes once upon a time. Here's what's going on in the world. We're very concerned about obesity and diabetes in America. The food industry's bad and it's causing all this." Shane likens the launch of Health Warrior to an Indiana Jones–type adventure, with business soul mates along for the ride. "We were truly just having fun with it."

In Fact, Have a Blast!

How much fun is it figuring out your passions? Apparently, it's more fun if you belong to the younger generations. According to a Salesforce study in 2019, millennials and Gen Zers are 188 percent more likely to have the aim of creating a side business, compared to baby boomers or traditionalists.[10]

This goes to show, once again, how *essential* it is that you allow your team to pursue their side hustles—especially those who are millennials or Gen Zers. A happy team member is a more productive team member and letting them chase their passions could prove to be an invaluable decision.

Then again, you might be 75 years old with no millennials on your team to "whisper" to (not everyone can be like me … fortunately). No matter what, it's important to understand that finding your passions shouldn't be a source of stress. You don't find a passion because you've been forced into a corner, feel miserable with what you do, and are desperately trying to escape your currency. You find a passion by identifying something you enjoy doing and then having fun with your relentless pursuit of it.

The Case for Balance

The most balanced person I know is Marc Hodulich, who is perhaps best known for pioneering the "Beer Mile" (four laps around a track, four cans of beer). But his real accomplishments lie in the way he manages to work and live life to the fullest while remaining as cool as a can of Coors.

A track and field star at Auburn University, Marc's main venture, with Jesse Itzler, is 29029 Everesting, which gives participants 36 hours over a weekend to climb a total of 29,029 feet above sea level (the height of Everest) by walking up and down the side of a mountain. *Outside* magazine calls it "a highly social weekend of walking up mountains until you drop" in Idaho, Utah, and Ver-

---

10   "Five Small Business Statistics for 2019," Small Business Trends, June 20, 2019, https://smallbiztrends.com/2019/06/small-business-statistics-for-2019.html.

mont. Marc has been successful in many businesses. He's helped others build successful businesses. And he's done it all while managing to prioritize his two children and wife over anything else. Also note, Marc and Jesse recently sold 29029 to the fitness brand iFIT, which owns NordicTrack and other enterprises.

How does he maintain such a balance between business and family success? Balance, I've learned from Marc and many of the other people I interviewed for this book, begins with mindset. The more we wire our brains to prioritize and categorize the millions of choices facing us, the more those neurons will fire in the right direction. "The balanced living mindset allows us to incorporate and combine different aspects of living to create the ideal life for ourselves," writes Mark Lynch, founder of The Excellence Addiction.[11] "Since we are all different, with unique skills and interests, each of us will need to combine the different domains of living in different ways to achieve our ideal life. Which makes sense right? Obviously, the ideal lifestyle for an individual who wants to travel the world will differ from someone who wants to develop their own business empire. Regardless of exactly what you want to be or what you want to do/achieve in your life, you will have a balanced living mindset that will facilitate your successful attainment of these goals."

Abundant Thinking

Remember when boxes of cereal had prizes inside? Sugar Crisp had the toy submarine powered by baking powder while you could find Ghost Detectors at the bottom of an Apple Jacks box. When I was growing up in suburban Massachusetts in the 1980s, my four brothers, sister, and I were obsessed with an adventure game we

---

11   Mark Lynch, "Balanced Living Mindset Introduction," The Excellence Addiction, December 28, 2018, https://www.theexcellenceaddiction.com/balanced-living-mindset/.

could play after devouring bowls of Cap'n Crunch with ice-cold milk. Some of us were more obsessed than others.

Around the same time, Stephen Covey was writing *The 7 Habits of Highly Successful People: Powerful Lessons in Personal Change,* in which he coined the term "abundance mindset," defining it as "a concept in which a person believes there are enough resources and successes to share with others." Clearly, my brother Alex had an abundance mindset when it came to the Cap'n Crunch as he came up with a strategy for all of us to share the prizes. My sister, Sarah, operated with a scarcity mindset, displaying destructive and unnecessary competition as she rifled through box after box for the prizes inside. She failed to see how we could *all* win if we pooled our resources and found the treasures together.

(Sarah is now an abundant thinker and came up with one of my favorite lines about the power of our mindset: "Conviction is confidence plus clarity." It also helps that she edited this book, so was able to sneak this in.)

"The currency of real networking is not greed but generosity." —**Keith Ferrazzi**

Many studies show the benefits of having an abundance mindset over a scarcity mindset—and not just when it comes to the surprises inside cereal boxes. "Not having enough of what one needs has long been shown to have detrimental consequences for decision making," write the authors of a 2019 study in the *Proceed-*

ings of the National Academy of Sciences.[12] "Recent work suggests that the experience of insufficient resources can create a 'scarcity' mindset; increasing attention toward the scarce resource itself, but at the cost of attention for unrelated aspects."

In other words, when we're selfish about our asks, we do a terrible job of actually doing the asking. Scarcity mindsets turn us into askholes. They also wreck our ruthless pursuits of passion, as the aforementioned study continues. "When in a scarcity mindset compared with an abundance mindset, participants had increased activity in the orbitofrontal cortex, a region often implicated in valuation processes," reveal the researchers. "Moreover, again compared with abundance, a scarcity mindset decreased activity in the dorsolateral prefrontal cortex, an area well known for its role in goal-directed choice. This effect was predominant in the group of participants who experienced scarcity following abundance, suggesting that the effects of scarcity are largest when they are compared with previous situations when resources were plentiful."

10 Steps to Develop an Abundance Mindset & Mentality[13]

If you struggle with mindset, I highly recommend a piece Nicolette Stinson wrote for developing an abundance mindset and mentality on the Chopra website. I've added my own thoughts and suggestions, below.

---

12   Inge Huijsmans et al., "A Scarcity Mindset Alters Neural Processing Underlying Consumer Decision Making," *Proceedings of the National Academy of Sciences* 116, no. 24 (June 11, 2019): 11699–704, https://www.pnas.org/content/116/24/11699.

13   Nicolette Stinson, "10 Steps to Develop an Abundance Mindset," *Chopra* (blog), September 23, 2019, https://www.chopra.com/articles/10-steps-to-develop-an-abundance-mindset.

1. Recognize the Power of Your Thoughts

"Cultivating mindfulness can help decipher when your thoughts are creating a mindset of scarcity or of abundance," writes Stinson, who suggests, if you find you are getting less than amazing results in any area of life, you should ask yourself, "Are my thoughts about this based in fear and scarcity?" If so, determine how you can shift your mindset to abundance.

2. Practice Gratitude

"Keep a gratitude journal and write down what you are genuinely grateful for every day," writes Stinson. "Aim to record at least 10 items. If you get stuck, remember to list the simple things that often get overlooked such as the bed you sleep in, a hot shower, the clean air you breathe, or just the chance to live another day."

When I began keeping my own gratitude journal, I went from seeing pollen on my car to seeing the amazing blossoms on the trees.

3. Believe the Sky's the Limit

If you're too tied up focusing on one particular blossom, however, you lose sight of the rest of the flowers opening up their petals. "The enemy of abundance is a contracted awareness," writes Stinson. "It is vital to loosen the mind's focus and create an expanded awareness that fosters the abundance mentality." This can happen through meditation or simply finding somewhere quiet and peaceful to spend a few minutes each day.

4. Cultivate and Share Your Passions and Purpose

"Understanding and creating confidence in the things you are both great at and love to do is an excellent way to foster belief in yourself," writes Stinson. "Learn how to share your gifts and provide value by serving those who would benefit most. Confidently share what you do through a personal brand presence online or in person."

As Lydia Fenet says, the most important trait of successful networkers is confidence. *Every* person around you needs to know your purpose!

5. Develop Mastery Experiences

These are your primary passions—the ones you're practicing daily that will automatically give you an abundance mindset. "If you get one percent better at something each day," writes Stinson, "then a year later you will be 365 percent better and will have created a mastery experience."

6. Pick Your Words Wisely

"The language you use, as well as what you tell yourself and others, shapes your reality," writes Stinson. "Are you telling stories of scarcity or stories of abundance?"

You might say, for example, "I can't have a beer because I stopped drinking last year." That's a scarcity mentality. Speaking from an abundance mentality would be, "I've chosen to kick alcohol out of my life, and it's the best decision I've ever made."

7. Build Beyond a Growth Mindset

"Become curious about other people and their experiences," writes Stinson. "Have an intention to ask someone every day about their life, what their goals are, and how they plan to achieve them. Practice simply listening to their answers and learning from what they have to say instead of talking about your life or offering your own advice. Then, reflect on your own beliefs about your ability and the abilities of those around you to change and grow."

8. Think Like a Beginner

Beginners have an automatic willingness to override close-mindedness because they need an open mind in order to learn something. Even if you're an expert, maintaining an attitude of openness and enthusiasm will create an abundance mindset.

9. Notice the Good!

"The next time you have a perceived problem or something doesn't seem to be going right, look at the problem from a larger, more holistic perspective," writes Stinson. "Instead of focusing on what is going wrong and trying to fix the problem, focus instead on what is actually going right as it relates to the topic and brainstorm ways to support that even further."

10. Speak Daily Abundance Affirmations

"Research from Carnegie Mellon University," reports Stinson, "suggests that the use of positive affirmations can improve problem-solving skills and decrease signs of stress." She suggests making a list of any fears you have, and what you think is going to happen from your voice of fear and scarcity. "Then, write down the opposite of what your fears are or what you deeply desire," writes Stinson. "Use the second list as your own personal list of daily affirmations."

Embracing the Grey Area and Dropping your FU Backpack

If you're as impatient as I am, chances are you want to jump on every opportunity, especially after reading this book. But we have to embrace what I call the "grey area" as we evolve our currencies. The grey area is the time period during which our currencies evolve when people still know us by our old currencies even though we are investing so much time and attention trying to become known for our new currencies.

A few months after I published a bestselling book on culture and connection, people were still coming to me for advice on digital and social media—my *old* currency. I expressed my frustration over coffee with Paul Ollinger, a good friend who was one of the original people at Facebook and is now a comedian, author, and podcast host of *Crazy Money with Paul Ollinger*. Paul told me to "drop your 'FU backpack' at the door." In other words, celebrate the fact you even have a job right now and accept your currency until demand for the new one picks up. This was one of the most important pieces of advice I'd ever received because it allowed me to embrace my role at my advertising agency and to instead use my evolving currency to open up doors (which soon became my full-time job).

In an article for *Forge,* Paul dives into some of the issues professionals later in their career might face as they find themselves both overworked and uninspired:

"First, honor the gravity of the situation by hiring a therapist or a professional coach with whom you can explore potential solutions. You should be talking about your problem, but not with me or on social media, or even to your partner if you find yourself complaining ad nauseam.

"Second, though your problem feels urgent, summon patience. A thoughtful change will take time—years, perhaps—to reduce burn rate, reposition yourself professionally, or find a more hospitable work home. Lawyers can secure in-house positions on the client-side. Financial and consulting types can explore CFO, controller, or strategy positions. Not that these jobs are cakewalks, but they generally come with a more manageable lifestyle and a direct connection to an ongoing concern.

"Lastly, check your personal strength. When you're stressed at work, you need to have your best personal game going. Tap the brakes on the booze. Carve out time to get to the gym. And check where you're spending your energy at work. If a political battle presents itself, ask yourself whether the time and focus required to engage it will enrich or deplete you.

"Along these lines, be careful not to blow yourself up. Every day may feel like a crisis, but it's not. You're in a good place. Recall that the job you have today is a gig you once dreamed of. You looked up to the person who held your current position and today there are dozens of younger people who hold you in admiration. (Note: Don't sleep with them.)"[14]

We *must* embrace the grey area as we evolve our currencies and drop that FU backpack at the door.

It's Not Just about You

Sometimes we can get so focused on what *we* need that the rest of the world seems to fade to black as we chase that sparkly, rainbow-colored connection until we're completely out of breath. It reminds me of my friend Sasha who used to train for marathons *only on the treadmill.* He was working as a rep for a pharmaceutical company and was often overseas in France, Brazil, Russia, and beyond. Every day, he'd wake up at 5 a.m. and find a gym, no matter where he was traveling, and stake his claim to a treadmill with his trusty water bottle. Once his music (the same Spotify playlist, of course) was playing through his AirPods, Sasha would hit go and not stop until he'd logged 8, 16, or 22 miles.

---

14   Paul Ollinger, "Mid-Career Burnout Is Real," *Forge* (blog), *Medium*, April 22, 2021, https://forge.medium.com/mid-career-burnout-is-real-8be4f2ddcea8.

Can you imagine running 22 miles on a treadmill? But that's essentially what we're doing when we lose sight of networking as the process of building mutually beneficial connections and instead start thinking, "How can I make this work for me?" Sure, Sasha ended up rocking his marathons, even qualifying for Boston, but every time I think of him, I imagine how much more fun it would be to run different routes and meet new people along the way as he ran by the Eiffel Tower, along the beaches of Rio, or through the city streets of Moscow.

Perhaps no city is a better example of networking's power than Washington, D.C., where Rory Cooper has worked as a lobbyist for more than two decades.

"The way you get your first internship and your first job in Washington is by somebody saying, 'Here are four people you should speak with who might be able to help,'" says Rory. "And then when you talk to those four people, you ask them if there's anybody else that they think you should talk to. I remember doing that when I was 21 years old and connected with a lobbyist for Johnson Controls. I thanked him for having the informational meeting, and he said, 'Well, I just remember when I did this when I was your age.' That has stuck with me for the last 22 years. Any time anybody has ever asked me, like, 'Hey, I know this young person, would you mind speaking to them?' I've never said no. I've never, ever, ever said no to a request to sit down with the young person or even somebody who's career transitioning and is a peer and help them sort through it because that has come back to reward me a million times over. The more you help build people up, the more it really does benefit you in the long term. It makes you feel good because you know you know that you had an impact."

No One-Size-Fits-All Approach to Motivation

What motivates you more, the desire for success or the fear of failure? You might be surprised by your answer if you give yourself some time to consider your motivations.

When writing this book, I talked with Nike's Laurie Randall. Laurie's one of the most driven, successful, and brilliant people I know. I've had the honor of connecting with her and witnessing a small fraction of what she does. In one of those encounters, we got to talking about how she keeps motivated and overcomes some of the negative events in her life.

"I have a 24-hour rule—maybe I need to shorten it to two," Laurie told me. "But I always tell myself that I have one day to mope about negative events in life. Once I recognize that I can't change the outcome, I make myself move on."

As a "super competitive" person working at such a high-profile company, Laurie still can't shake her fear of failure after 10 years at Nike. "The people who work here are incredibly intelligent and driven. So my fear of failure is actually motivating for me."

A lot of people feel just like Laurie, although some of them won't admit it. They *think* a drive for success pushes them forward when the truth is that they are more afraid to fail than they are driven for success. Why is that important? Because you can make better decisions when you know what actually motivates you. For example, if Laurie were more motivated by a drive for success than a fear of failure, she likely wouldn't need a 24-hour rule for when things go wrong. She'd be so driven by success that temporary failures wouldn't cause her to mope. But she knows that she fears failure and that negative events could trigger fears and moping that could last for days. Thus, she created an objective 24-hour rule that helps her refocus, similar to my two-hour rule, which I mentioned earlier in the book.

There's nothing better or worse about being motivated by a drive for success versus fear of failure. The key is to understand what motivates you so you can set up the right responses when things go wrong.

"Some people are burned out and fatigued by their work when you try to connect with them. But others are really invested. I pick up on that energy. You're not always gonna get it right. But I do feel like you kind of got to make the first move. It's like dating. I'd say 20 percent of the time, it goes sideways, but overwhelmingly, it goes well. You've got to trust your gut—your Spidey sense." —**Cary Franklin**

Don't Take Rejection Personally

Finally, when chasing something big, you *are* going to get rejected. You will ask too soon. You will hit obstacles. You will stumble. There is nothing you can do about it.

When that happens, it's natural to take every "no" personally, like there's something wrong with you. It's not easy for me, either, as I keep aiming higher and higher. In my conversation with former NFL player and current Nike performance coach, Alex Molden, I learned quite a bit about rejection.

Alex knows rejection. After all, he went from being the No. 11 overall draft pick in the first round of the 1996 NFL draft to finding himself unemployed and unable to get a job in 2003. Years later, he still experiences rejection. He's heard "no" quite a bit.

"What I've become really good at is separating that 'no' from emotions," he says. "Sure, I guess I get wrapped up in the idea that *maybe they don't like me or don't like how I look.* But the reality is, that person probably said no because it wasn't the right time to say yes to whatever I was proposing."

There's a lot of wisdom in that last sentence—so much so that I wanted to end this mindset chapter with it. If you struggle with taking every "no" personally, is it possible that you view the word "no" as permanent? As fatal?

For example, assume you are at a coffee meeting with a local entrepreneur. She's extremely successful, and you ask if she'd be willing to connect you with a friend of hers. She says no. Maybe you asked too early. Maybe you have asked for more than you've given. Who knows what the reason is. You have no idea why.

When many people don't know why someone says "no," they immediately conclude that there has to be something wrong with them and that the "no" is permanent. But what if the issue really *was* just a comfort level? What if you hadn't given enough before making the ask? What if, instead of never asking this entrepreneur for coffee again and assuming you blew your ask, you just started giving? What if you saved your asks for a number of months, or even longer, and just focused on building an authentic relationship with her?

Chances are, that "no" will eventually turn into a "yes" and that it really wasn't a permanent "no" but a "not yet."

TL;DR

Double down on developing a growth mindset and develop the ability to see a bright future for yourself. Embrace resilience and tenacity. My favorite quote is "The best is yet to come," and this is also true for you!

Make the Connection

- Establishing new relationships makes us smarter—and also requires a growth mindset.
- Practice resilience and tenacity when creating connections.
- Slowing down and refueling can be the best way to get our currencies and passions back on track.
- As Shane Emmett says, the best way to start side hustles is as a hobby, where you're having fun with it. And then the initial market is your friends and family. Word of mouth will tell you whether you should spend money on it or not.
- When we're selfish about our asks, we do a terrible job of actually doing the asking.

CHAPTER 8:

Your Heart

Recently, my friend Alan volunteered to coach his seven-year-old's basketball team. There was just one problem: He had never played organized basketball in his life. He didn't know a single basketball drill. He had no idea how to shoot a basketball. In fact, he was so bad at basketball that once he began coaching, he never actually shot a basketball during any practice or game out of fear that the kids would lose all faith in their coach.

But Alan did two important things to keep his team motivated and competitive in every game that season.

First, he realized the seven-year-olds wouldn't shoot if the defender's hand was in their field of vision. So he instructed his team to "just raise one hand like you want to ask the teacher a question" when they're on defense. Sure enough, his team became masterful at defending one-on-one.

Second, he told his team to not worry about basketball if they didn't know what to do on the court. "If you get stuck out there, don't worry. We all get stuck. We worry about what our hands are doing," said Alan. "We worry about what our feet are doing. We worry about whether we are in the right spot. We worry about so many things. I don't want you to worry about any of those things. I just want you to focus on two muscles—the two *strongest* muscles in our bodies."

Alan told the kids these are our hustle muscles: our heads and our hearts. "Whenever you don't know what to do on the court … whenever you feel tired … whenever you feel worried … or when you make a mistake … or when you miss a shot or a pass gets stolen … because *all* of those things *will* happen … I want you to focus on just two things: your hustle muscles … your head and your heart," he said. "Those two muscles are more powerful than *anything* you will face on the court this entire season. They're stronger than the biggest defender. They're faster than the fastest guy on the other team. They're smarter than the most well-designed play. And they are *all* you need to think about to get through anything on the court. Just those two things. Just your hustle muscles. All they do is help. Your head keeps you focused. It points you in the right direction. Your heart is like your motor. Your engine. It keeps you going. It can push you through when you're exhausted or even worried."

Using your hustle muscles became a theme for the team, which soon became known as one of the most driven in the league, even as it lost game after game.

During one memorable game, the team was losing again with just a minute to go. One of the kids had the ball in his hands when a second defender approached him for a double team. As he looked for teammates to help out, one of the kids on the bench delivered my friend's greatest memory of the season when, seemingly out of nowhere, he started yelling "HUSTLE MUSCLES!!!!!" over and over again at the top of his lungs. My friend literally can't remember much about the season and doesn't even remember what happened after that kid started screaming. He knows the team ended up winning as many games as they lost. They were beaten badly in a couple of games but were in most games until the end. But he chokes up about this day knowing that each of those kids left the season with the foundation to endure any challenge they will face if they can just remember to use their "hustle muscles."

The truth is that we can achieve whatever we want in our business or personal lives when our minds are focused and our hearts are pushing us forward toward something about which we are passionate.

In the last chapter, I talked all about the headwork we need to build a strong, healthy mindset. In this chapter, I'll talk about what we can do to make networking easier and better for us.

Some of this might make you feel uncomfortable at first. But I promise you that it's designed to get easier. And if you ever feel frustrated, just remember: Everything from here to the back of the book is the details. They are the strategies to help you achieve a future that is bigger and better than you ever imagined. They are designed to build deep connections with supporters and super-connectors. They are designed to turn *you* into a super-connector to attract even more supporters and super-connectors.

Remember, your head points you in the right direction and your heart keeps you going. You can figure out the rest. And you'll have this book on your shelf to help.

Putting in the Reps

As a former pro athlete, Alex Molden hits the gym—a lot.

"It's important to keep working on your muscles because we use them every day, and if you don't use them, they will become weak and inefficient," says Molden, adding that the exact same holds true when it comes to pursuing your passions and connecting with others. "Like having a solid training program to be in great shape for your sport, you have to start with a focused game plan!"

This includes

- Warm-up.
- Mobility (working on deficiencies).
- Working on the big muscles first then the little ones (stabilizers).
- Conditioning—the not-so-glamorous part of training. But that conditioning is what drives you to reach your goals.

Like at a gym, your networking muscles need to get worked over and over again. In fact, the work never stops. That's why it's so important for you to be passionate about your currency. Your passion leads to your efforts. You wake up when it's cold. You keep going when you hit an obstacle. You won't give up. And when your currency has value in the world you want to pursue, the currency helps you build momentum in the right direction. The combination of the two leads to results beyond your wildest dreams over time.

That's why the people who end up in the best physical health are those who are passionate about diet and exercise, the currency that makes them healthier. Their passion makes it easy for them to do the things that build momentum to a fitter body and healthier life.

Your passion will get you to do the work that gets you in front of the right people to push you closer to your goals.

So the first thing you must ask yourself is, "Am I passionate about my currency?" If the answer is "yes," then your passions will help you build momentum and push you along. If the answer is "no," you're out of alignment and will likely not build the momentum you want. It's essential that you incubate a passion or side hustle that is something *outside* of your day-to-day currency.

And there are two types of passions you're going to be building and incubating.

Passion 1

This passion is the on-deck circle or next in line to help you expand upon or reinvent your currency. It's something you'll be practicing either daily or weekly. For me, it was writing a book on millennials, which became my main currency within nine months. This is an example of an "unconnected passion" because my passions had evolved. The role of the passion project doesn't have to be to replace your currency; it's to lessen the dependence of your fulfillment entirely on your day-to-day job.

As an example of an "adjacent passion," I have a good friend who's a dentist and he absolutely loves what he does. He recognized that he had a need for new revenue lines as well as an interest in real estate. His Passion 1 became buying the real estate for his practice as they expanded.

Another example of an "adjacent passion" is my friend Bert who's one of the most successful morning radio show hosts in the U.S. His currency is "using his voice to draw listeners in and keeping them engaged and wanting more." Bert's Passion 1 became a podcasting network and consultancy where he coaches podcasters and radio hosts to be more engaging and entertaining while growing digital revenue.

An example of an "unconnected passion" is my going from the digital and social guy to the culture guy at my agency.

Passion 2

This is a hobby or something that brings you joy. The purpose of Passion 2 is to create something for yourself that practices some of that neuroplasticity (see chapter 2) in your brain. This could be learning to play an instrument, practicing a new language, or taking on a new sport (kiteboarding, anyone?) Most of these will *remain* hobbies that will also help you create connections with others. I can't think of what would happen if I tried to be a kiteboarding instructor because I'd most likely get frustrated and bored after just one week.

Embracing the Grey

When you create an "unconnected passion" to your currency, it's important you practice patience. Most passions take *at least three years* to curate. As you're doing it, you'll be asked for help or work that's still in line with your existing currency. It's absolutely essential that in these scenarios you continue to fulfill your currency and job duties.

When to Declare Your Passion as Your New Currency

People will say, "You will know when it's time." I like to look at it more prescriptively—it's not until you're making more momentum, connections, or money with a passion than with your currency that you can completely declare your passion as your currency.

The Power of Putting in the Reps

Before COVID-19, my friend Joy danced like Elaine on *Seinfeld*, Carlton on *The Fresh Prince of Bel-Air*, and the worst celebrities you can imagine on *Dancing with the Stars*. We called her special style of dancing "the broken seagull."

It's okay for me to share this because now Joy is a seriously amazing dancer, busting out the moves to everything from the Ying Yang Twins and Sia to Paula Abdul and Run DMC. That's because she's spent months learning to dance through an online workout. When she discovered an alternative to lifting weights and yoga, Joy was hooked on the energetic instructors and super-fun music. Before she knew it, she was dancing two or more hours a day, watching the same videos over and over and over and over again. Joy would pick one particular class for the day and practice for 30 minutes in front of her bathroom mirror, then 45 minutes at the gym before a final 45 minutes in her home office. I'm incredibly impressed—and way too intimidated to hit the dance floor with Joy.

This is the power of reps.

In *Outliers,* Malcolm Gladwell wrote about the 10,000-hour rule, which actually originated from a Florida State University professor who studied high-performing people and found the more time they spent, the better they got. But here's the thing: you don't need 10,000 hours to reap the benefits of reps! It was only the very top athletes, musicians, and chess grandmasters who spent somewhere around 10,000 hours practicing their craft, found the FSU professor.

"A society-wide game of telephone started to be played," explains Josh Kaufman in a TED Talk. "So this message, it takes 10,000 hours to reach the top of an ultracompetitive field, became 'it takes 10,000 hours to become an expert at something' which became 'it takes 10,000 hours to become good at something' which became 'it takes 10,000 hours to learn something.'"

Instead, as Kaufman discovered, it takes only about 20 hours of deliberate, dedicated practice to get really good at something (as he demonstrates by playing a medley of songs on his ukulele).

"With a little bit of practice," says Kaufman, "you get really good really quick."

Practice Makes Progress

Ukuleles aside (*please!*), scholarly research has proven the power of repetition, with no specific number of hours attached. The point is, you can become an expert at creating genuine connections—whether you want to hit your sales cycle goals or move from working the floor of Kohl's department store to manager—by simply practicing. This means, for our purposes, using some of the basics I've presented throughout this book:

- Create your personal brand
- Focus on setting goals
- Practice reciprocity
- Mask your ask in your dream

Innate talent? Nope, effort.

"We agree that expert performance is qualitatively different from normal performance and even that expert performers have characteristics and abilities that are qualitatively different from or at least outside the range of those of normal adults," write the authors of a *Psychological Review* article. "However, we deny that these differences are immutable, that is, due to innate talent. Only a few exceptions, most notably height, are genetically prescribed. Instead, we argue that the differences between expert performers and normal adults reflect a life-long period of deliberate effort to improve performance in a specific domain. Most of our scientific knowledge about improvement and change comes from laboratory studies of training and practice that lasted hours, days, and occasionally weeks and months."[15]

Keep 'Em in the Loop!

In chapter 4, I shared a conversation I had with NFL legend Larry Fitzgerald. I mentioned how important it is to keep people updated once they've connected you with someone else. Astor Chambers also points out that when we connect with super-connectors, we have a responsibility to keep them up to date on our progress.

When I hear from someone I've helped, I can live vicariously through their wins instead of wondering what happened to them. There's nothing worse than giving an introduction to someone and then wondering how it turned out or whether or not those people ever connected.

Remember, super-connectors like me get *highs* by making connections happen, so allow us to live vicariously by bringing us along. Give me that dopamine fix I forever crave by being a catalyst to connection!

But Chris, This Is Painful!

I get it. Practice is a pain in the butt sometimes. Even the most dedicated people I know whine about another hour on the piano or yet another day of working on their personal brand (trust me, tattoos hurt). Or what happens when you're meeting with an amazing prospect who might introduce you to Warren Buffett—and she has an annoying habit of picking her teeth with her pinky nail?

---

15 K. Anders Ericsson, Ralf Th. Krampe, and Clemens Tesch-Römer, "The Role of Deliberate Practice in the Acquisition of Expert Performance," *Psychological Review* 100, no. 3 (1993): 363–406, https://graphics8.nytimes.com/images/blogs/freakonomics/pdf/DeliberatePractice(PsychologicalReview).pdf.

Four words: Focus on something else. My dancer-friend Joy, for example, focuses on the feet of her instructors when their flailing arms are driving her nuts or when they play a song by Pink. During Zoom calls, you can look around at their background (also good for research); in person, shift your gaze to their eyes or just use your imagination to take you to an Emily Post world of good etiquette.

Every single day, you should be practicing or learning around your first passion. Surprisingly, one of the most efficient ways of doing this is to write a book. I try to encourage *everyone* I meet to write a book. It's also a great exercise if you get stuck in determining your passions to answer the question, "If you could write one book, what would that book be about?" Having now written two books, I've become an expert on how to write a book and build an ecosystem around it because I immersed myself in the process and hired experts for each aspect.

It's also super important that you talk about your passions. This will make you more interesting in your conversations and will give you other topics for you to connect with prospects and customers about. When I first reached out to the author Jon Acuff for advice for my first book, he said. "Chris, it's all about reps—take every interview, even if it's a podcast with only five listeners; with reps you'll become an expert." He was right.

Alignment, Assignment, Adjustment

After being a first-round draft pick in the NFL, Alex Molden received some tools from his coach, Willie Shaw. Alex was fast, strong, and he could listen and learn, said Willie, but he needed more for great success and being able to play a long time. "Alignment, assignment, adjustment," Alex recalls of the three things Willie said would change his world. He would have to be aligned with everybody else on the team or they would be beaten before the ball was even snapped. Alex would have to know his assignment inside out and backward. "Alex, on every play, in every situation, whatever team you're going to be on, it's your job to know your job." And Alex would always need a backup to the backup plan, an ability to pivot whenever the opponents shifted formations or motioned their offensive skill players.

"I started looking at it from his eyes—alignment, assignment, adjustment," says Alex, who began to apply these three fundamentals to every situation in his life. "It gave me great success on the field, and it also gave me confidence off the field. So much confidence that when I stepped away from football—it was scary and I was depressed—I said to myself, 'What can I depend on?' And the answer was alignment, assignment, adjustment." His alignment was his faith, his family, and his career. His assignment was his purpose, which led him to become a performance trainer for Nike. And Alex's adjustments have come from recognizing his passions of public speaking and coaching people on leadership. "I know there's an impact," he says. "I can help people become better leaders, and not just in the corporate world. If I'm helping you become a better leader, a better influencer, it should be across all boards."

Alex shows us that no matter where you are in your job, figure out what you are learning in that currency that can parlay to other parts of your life. As I told Alex, we're all constantly reiterating what we're doing to accommodate our evolving purposes and bring our currencies along with that.

Stay Curious

Almost every good decision I've made, from agreeing to meet a woman named Julie who would become my wife to bringing kids into our life has been made out of curiosity. What would it be like to kiteboard the Keys? What charities can I give back to? The same is true of my relationships. I'm naturally curious about the man I see stocking the Publix shelves with Peet's Coffee, and I'm naturally curious about everyone I've interviewed for this book from Alexander Gilkes to Vincent Pugliese.

"People love talking about themselves. Just ask questions."
—**Alexander Gilkes**

Curiosity is one of the most important networking "muscles" we must keep working repeatedly. As Francesca Gino shows in a *Harvard Business Review* article, curiosity means fewer decision-making errors, more innovation, and better performance, among other enormous benefits. It naturally gives us the empathy to connect with others.

"My research found that curiosity encourages members of a group to put themselves in one another's shoes and take an interest in one another's ideas rather than focus only on their own perspective," writes Gino. "That causes them to work together more effectively and smoothly: Conflicts are less heated, and groups achieve better results."[16]

---

16 Francesca Gino, "The Business Case for Curiosity," *Harvard Business Review*, September 1, 2018, https://hbr.org/2018/09/the-business-case-for-curiosity.

Business Is a Byproduct of Connection

I was recently helping an amazing leader Kris Strouthopoulos, who was introduced to me via Alexandra Wilkis Wilson after we connected to interview her for this book. Kris has an amazing lingerie brand called Giapenta, and I helped introduce her to a bunch of investors (a handful of whom invested). She called me one day and said, "Chris, what I can do for you?" I immediately replied, "You don't have to do anything. I believe in you and want you to succeed. I've been so impressed by your product but also your tenacity and resilience. I want you to win and seeing you win is enough." I truly believe that in the future a byproduct of this connection and help will be us doing business together.

But it's not just helping her out that created our connection. A friend pointed out to me that much of my connection with others comes from my ability to run the full spectrum of conversation. I also tell many people that my ability to do this is that I'm not the slightest bit scared to embrace the empathetic and feminine side of my persona as much as the masculine side.

"True connection happens when there are no guards, there's no image, there are no projections." —**Karissa Kouchis**

I'll tell whoever is willing to listen that even in my family I embody a ton of the typical feminine traits of sensitivity with my daughters that most men don't go near. I also run my business life in the same realm. And yes, I do have a tattoo on my left arm that has a band for feminine energy and a band for masculine energy that I wear with the utmost pride.

Curiosity for the Cutco Rep

"It's courage, creativity, and curiosity that will get us to the emotion," says Justin Janowski, founder and CEO of Faith2Influence, explaining how these attributes are especially beneficial for salespeople. (Justin, by the way, is a master at advising on the shorter sales cycles. My strengths are more in longer, high-dollar sales cycles.) "Be deeply curious about your prospects; keep asking the next curious question. 'Why, why, why, why?' It will be four or five layers deeper than the surface-level answer that came first. That's where the leverage is. And if we're courageous enough to stay there with them and curiously ask the next question instead of moving on, we're going to have a lot more success."

Curiosity is the difference between networking and connecting.

By now, most of us have read and heard parables about the power of Cutco knives, thanks to books such as John Ruhlin's *Giftology*. The beauty of selling this product, says Justin Janowski, is that there are many different ways to do it. According to Justin, the best sales reps on in-home appointments exude insatiable curiosity. As he explains, a Cutco rep could make the entire sales presentation all about kitchen knives or they could say: "Mrs. Jones, today I want to talk to you about your life in the kitchen, about your family, and about how you interact around food together.

Then, I want to hear your vision for what you'd like that to look like. After that, I'll share any recommendations I have of products or strategies that may be able to bring that vision to light and you can decide whether or not you want to act on those recommendations. Either way, my hope is that we end this meeting with you feeling a bit more energized about the three meals that you have every day and the way you engage with your family during those three meals. Does that sound good?"

By engaging in a genuine conversation with Mrs. Jones, the Cutco rep expresses natural curiosity about her family, making the emotional connection that ultimately seals the deal. She doesn't buy the knives—she buys the vision for her family.

This is the power of asking curious questions that dig deeper than the surface.

Talk to the Taxi Driver

"Those who are truly great at building cohorts around them are the people who have a true ability to immediately engender trust, and trust is the true anchor in any relationship," says Alexander Gilkes. "Trust ultimately comes from true benevolence. Your connection, and the trust, is not something that can be falsely engineered. It has to be an innate part of you if you're offering your currency."

Gilkes says that his own sense of trust comes from taking risks and being "hypercurious" in his approach to the world. "My brain is always taking in new information, seeing patterns, and seeking areas that I don't know," he says. "I'm just constantly in pursuit of trying to understand what I don't know. My vehicle to unearth the truth has always been human connection. I learn way more from people—engagement, interactions, and stories from people—than I do through the written word or anything else."

Living in many countries including Chile and Russia, Gilkes has learned languages with his hypercurious navigation through life. "I learned my Russian through just getting in taxis every single day where I used to be able to travel across to Saint Petersburg for half a dollar," he says. "And I would just pay someone to show me any part of town, and I would just talk to the taxi driver time and time again. And I build my confidence by asking about a favorite sports team or other cultural reference points. And it fuels my curiosity."

Bogdan Constantin has had similar success with his own curiosity while in cars. "One of the best conversations I ever had was in Minneapolis," he says. "My Uber driver was a lost boy from Sudan. I was able to ask him about his life growing up in the late 80s and early 90s in an orphanage. And here he was an Uber driver, thankful that he was in America, thankful that he could earn a living even after everything that he'd gone through. I was just naturally curious. I just wanted to learn. I wanted to connect with him."

Practice Being "Impatiently Patient"

Paul Brown is the CEO of Inspire Brands, which is the second-largest restaurant owner in the country. He attributes his success to being "impatiently patient"—which is terrific terminology as we navigate our currencies and passions and hit unknown areas.

The trick is turning just plain impatience (which Paul sees often, especially among younger generations) into something more productive. "There's an instant, instantaneous gratification factor today," he says, "as well as an impatience; people don't necessarily put in the time to make lateral moves to get experience and create a foundation. Inspire came out of slowly accumulating that experience, but also my tenacity in becoming successful and leading a more fulfilling life. I call it impatiently patient."

Driven to run his own company since he was 13, Paul was focused on creating something interesting and significant, not necessarily becoming the CEO of such a large business.

"There are some people I've met so focused on being a CEO that they jump at that opportunity, one could argue too quickly," says Paul. "And then they get stuck. I wanted to do something at scale, and I knew to do something at scale, I needed to actually get a large set of experiences operating at scale. I had to look for the right opportunity—the right platform, something that I would enjoy, but also something with which I can really make a significant change at a significant scale—impatiently patient."

Stay Playful

We have energy. All of us have energy. Sure, some (admittedly, including me) have way more energy than others, and some have less. This goes beyond the kind of energy we produce when we're riding the Peloton. (Though MIT researchers are working on 'harvesting human energy' from people riding stationary bikes.[17])

The great thing about energy is that people who have less energy can rely on people who have more energy. The key is to recognize energy levels and to work with them as you meet with prospects and connections. "Every time you have a conversation, you can lead it to a place where it's moving the needle closer to where you want it to go," explains Karissa Kouchis, adding how we often waste energy by forcing it the wrong way, like trying to fit

---

17 Ucilia Wang, "The Scientists Harvesting Energy from Humans to Power Our Wearables," *The Guardian*, February 4, 2016, https://www.theguardian.com/sustainable-business/2016/feb/04/harvesting-energy-humans-walking-charge-wearables-bending-mit.

a circle into a square. "You've got to be able to save your energy," she says. "So they invest all of their time in one thing."

When people are asking Karissa for something, she can sense this pent-up energy. "And I'm like, 'Screw that!'" she says of what she's thinking during such meetings. "'Let me move on because I could close seven deals with the energy that I see you putting into just a few words with me.'"

So how do we get the right amount of energy? Start being more playful, says Karissa. "If you're getting a 'no' and your brow is furrowed and you feel sick in your gut, you're not being playful, and no one wants to do business with someone uptight. If you're quick-witted and playful, I can tell you've done your inner work, and that you have an abundance mindset."

The secret of networking, says Karissa, is that you can't network until you've worked on yourself. "Work on yourself until you are so comfortable and sure of yourself and your unique value-add, and your currency, and what you're doing in the world, and you feel solid that you don't need to project or talk about who you are and what you do and how great you are," she says. "Just exist in who you are. That's when true organic networking happens. True connection happens when there are no guards, there's no image, there are no projections."

The Guy Who Wanted to Punch Me in the Face

Recently, I was speaking to an audience of about 30 men. We were brought there by my good friend Tommy Breedlove for one of his amazing Legendary Life retreats. I was giving one of those special speeches; Tommy always has the best people at his retreats, and I found myself able to really harness everyone's energy.

It was also one of the first times that I bridged the content from my first book *The Millennial Whisperer* with this new content that you're reading. In other words, it was one of the first speeches I combined the tactics for creating connections with your employees with the tactics and importance of connection outside of your organization.

I've done enough speeches to read the energy in a room. During almost any speech, there's always a handful of people who look like they want to punch me in the face. They're usually the ones with a scowl on their face and their arms crossed. In this particular speech, it was easy to pick the guy out. He was sitting on the left side of the room and didn't really move away from this pose.

But afterward, I had the chance to speak with this guy, who will remain nameless to protect his identity, over dinner. The guy looked to be in his midfifties. He was conservatively dressed and came across as pretty corporate in nature.

The first thing I told him was that I could tell he was the guy in the audience who wanted to punch me in the face. I wanted to ask about what pissed him off the most. He was standing across from me as I asked him this and was taken aback at first, but then he immediately responded. "I did want to punch you in the face," he said, "but the reason is different than you might think. Everything you said up there goes against all that I've learned in my career and my first reaction was to reject it but as I really listened, it intrigued me. You made me realize I have 20 years of credibility and trust built up, and now I'm thinking about how to enjoy it. I also work for Microsoft and I want to talk to you about how I can put some of your points in action for the younger people who I really respect."

I suggested we hop on a phone call the following Friday, and we put it on our calendars for 3 p.m. That phone call was one of the best phone calls I've ever had. We spoke for over an hour, half sharing our commonalities of both quitting drinking at age

36 and so much more (I hate phone calls and I never wanted this one to end). We decided that we should do this *every* Friday. Now, six months later, we talk *every* Friday afternoon, and the guy who wanted to punch me in the face has turned into one of my closest confidants. He's one of two people to whom I gave this book to do their own editing. Sometimes, we'll talk every day of the week. The other day, he even sent me this …

"The first time I listened to you speak, you talked about work being fun and trying to figure out how food tastes by listening to someone describe it. I could not even fathom what that might feel like. Five months later, I feel exactly what you mean. This has been awesome. I would have never believed one person could change my view of work—and certainly not a guy with yellow glasses."

I was finally able to see the content of this book play out with someone and have a massive impact! Now I'm 1/1,000,000 of my way to my goal of helping 1,000,000 people!

TL;DR

Life *can* be a ruthless pursuit of passions, and most likely you don't have enough of them. Take action and start developing some of your passions and curiosities into something that can help you create momentum. You may surprise yourself with a multimillion-dollar side hustle!

Make the Connection

- Like at a gym, your networking muscles need to get worked over and over again. In fact, the work never stops. Start developing them today!
- It takes only about 20 hours of deliberate, dedicated practice to get good at something.

- To check in on your progress, think of alignment, assignment, adjustment.
- Every single day, you should be practicing or learning around your first passion. (One of the most efficient ways of doing that, believe it or not, is to write a book. Ask yourself, "What's the one book that I was meant to write?")
- Identify passions that you think you can spend 20 hours pursuing. If you've already done that, ask yourself if you can spend the next three years developing it as a side hustle.

PART 4:

MAKE IT HAPPEN

CHAPTER 9:

When to Go for the Ask

You've learned how *not* to network and the importance of saving your asks. You know the type of people you need in your support network. You have learned the importance of supporters and super-connectors—and the importance of becoming a super-connector.

You've learned the right mindset you need to approach connecting. You know how to build the muscles (and heart) you need to keep building toward achievements that are bigger than anything you believed possible.

Now what?

Now it's time to learn when—and how—to go in for the ask.

Now it's time to make it all happen.

Like in comedy, one of the most important rules of going for the ask is timing.

Develop impeccable comedic timing like Aziz Ansari and you, too, can go from crickets at an open mic night to selling out theaters and starring in a sitcom.

Develop impeccable networking timing like Alexandra Wilkis Wilson and you, too, can build the relationships that will take you from dreaming of a better life to achieving that seemingly elusive point in which passion, purpose, and profession collide.

The good news is that timing is more of an art than a science. There's no precise moment in time at which you either go for the ask or lose the opportunity. And you can generally not get into too much trouble asking too late, especially compared to the damage you can do by asking too early. So if you remember only one thing about timing, remember to err on the side of asking later than you could instead of earlier than you should.

The bad news is that this means there's generally no precise formula to follow. There's no 72-hour rule, like the one we used to follow to make sure we didn't look desperate after a date by calling too soon. But there *are* a number of things you can look for to know when the time is right to go for the ask. And that's exactly what I'm going to share with you for the rest of this chapter.

The Long Haul

When I proposed to my wife, Julie, I didn't just pop the question a couple of weeks after meeting her (as much as I wanted to). Instead, we spent months developing our relationship. Okay, it was only four months, but my point is: take your time. Sure, you're not getting married to this potential person in your network, but you are entering a relationship that should, if you play it right, last a lifetime.

The only time I go for the ask is when it's manifested around my own dreams and when it's to have a greater impact. No potential connection can help me work toward my dreams or make an impact if our relationship is brief or transactional. If you look at all the asks that you're tempted to make of people, I highly recommend taking a more patient strategy. Remember, we only have one ask for anyone we're developing a relationship with, and this happens *over time!* Instead of "dating" connections, you'll get more value by "marrying" them (not the way I married Julie, of course, but you get the point).

Sales Cycles

If you're in sales, you have to understand your sales cycle before you even begin to put a timetable on an ask. Some of my mentors and people in my network have short sales cycles—they're making 80,000 calls a year. This means they must go in for the ask early in their sales cycle, or they'll be scrambling by the end of it.

Let's say, for example, you're selling Scotch tape and you have an annual quota to fill. You just want to move that tape so you're not stuck with it at the end of the year (See what I did there?). So chances are you have little time to take your Scotch tape aficionado out for a glass of Glenfiddich. Just ask already: "It sounds like you tape a lot of *Garfield* cartoons to your fridge. Wouldn't a 12-pack of Scotch tape help?" It's a small ask. It's a short sales cycle. It's fine to ask once you establish a legitimate relationship.

Most of our jobs are now different from door-to-door selling. From Bombas socks to Warby Parker glasses, we're building relationships with our customers so they return to us repeatedly and for more than one product. And many people in the networking world are on long sales cycles. Aaron Abrahms may sell insurance, but he targets billionaires for his products. So this takes months, if not years; it's a far cry from someone trying to push a neatly tied up package of insurance through the front door. He's not asking people to buy insurance the first time he meets them.

Understand your sales cycle. Learn to recognize where people are in the sales cycle. Build rapport and add value while they move along the sales cycle. And ask when people are getting close to the end of the sales cycle.

When you pay attention to the sales cycle, you can build a bigger and more consistent pipeline because you don't push people out of your pipeline by asking too soon, instead consistently nurturing relationships with people who aren't ready to buy and only asking people to close sales once they get to the end of the natural sales cycle.

Wait as Long as Possible (But Not Too Long)

When is the right time in a relationship to go for the ask? "I say it's 10 percent after the time when you think you needed to go for the ask more than life itself," says Bogdan Constantin. "I try to wait as long as possible."

When Bogdan was teaching himself the best ways to become a successful entrepreneur, he studied psychology books laying out the basic premise that when we do good deeds for people, they often want to reciprocate those deeds. "They want to say thank you in some way and you don't even *have to* ask," says Bogdan. But the right time is when you absolutely think you're going to go crazy if you don't have it. And then you wait 10 percent more."

"Don't think about the outcome. The preparation and the process are what matters. With some people, the process takes weeks. With some people, it takes years. But the process is the fun part." —**Cary Franklin**

Understand Where You Stand on the "Ask Continuum"

In chapter 1, I introduced the concept of the "ask continuum."

If you recall, on one side of the continuum, it's super easy for you to go in for the ask and come across as an askhole. You ask too soon. You don't wait to build rapport. You don't wait to add much value. You just ask. And ask. And ask some more.

On the other side, you routinely let asks pass you by. You wait way too long and end up losing opportunity after opportunity.

Right in the middle is the sweet spot.

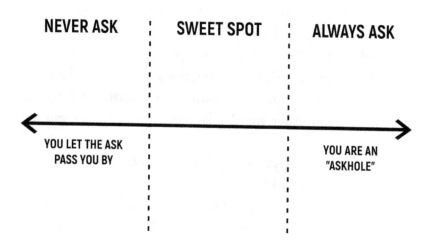

Save your asks on the left side. Tread carefully as you approach the middle. Ask when you get to the right. But don't misconstrue the title of this book as suggesting you should save your asks *forever*. You need to go in for an ask. But you just need to wait until the time is right. I go in for asks all the time. I just wait until I'm in the sweet spot to do so.

The concept of saving your asks is a controversial one in the networking world though. You hear people scream, "The squeaky wheel gets the oil" and "They can't say yes if you don't ask" and other phrases designed to encourage people to ask. I get it. Asking is important. Even the incredible Alexandra Wilkis Wilson told me she didn't like the title of my book at first. In her words, "I'm constantly advising strong, female entrepreneurs about the importance of the 'ask' itself."

I reassured her though that the title of the book isn't *Save Your Asks Forever*. It's about going in for lots of asks but just waiting until you've made a genuine connection to do so.

Don't Let Asks Pass You By

In late 2020, I participated in the Legendary Life retreat with several others led by Tommy Breedlove. I began discussing the ideas behind *Save Your Asks* with the group. During our barbecue lunch in the Atlanta wellness community of Serenbe, not knowing when he would see me again, Justin Janowski said, "Chris, you have to do a retreat for your book—this is too good for you not to do it."

So you must ask yourself, "When are the environment and energy ready for the ask?"

Justin—a guy who clearly doesn't find himself too far right on the "ask continuum"—chose that moment to pounce and asked me if I'd be interested in hiring him to help create a Save Your Asks summit and I jumped on it. I started planning my retreat right away—the first of many Save Your Asks summits. Justin helped Tommy create the Legendary Life retreat, so I had the pleasure of having had several high-value conversations with him before the summit. He had built rapport, added value, and showcased his work by helping Tommy.

Had he not asked, who knows if I would have started planning my own summit that soon. But his ask allowed me to push myself out of my comfort zone and start testing some of this book content in a two-day executive retreat. (It ended up being a roaring success.)

And had Justin not asked me to do that retreat in this setting, he could have let the ask pass him by because I likely would not have been in a room with him for a while after that. He had to capitalize on the energy created and us being face-to-face.

The Pain of Not Taking Action

"What stands in your way?" asks Justin Janowski. "What would life look like if you solved that one problem instead of wondering if you were good enough. If you had total confidence in your identity, who you were, and the value brought to the world, and you just felt light and free in that confidence—what would be possible from that place."

As Justin points out, we *must* have the confidence to understand who we are, what we stand for, and where we want to go. Confidence is one of the greatest traits of effective connecting, and unless you're connected to who you are, you'll just be faking it. If you don't do the work to understand what drives you as a human and what you're passionate about, you will be flying blind. Understand your purpose, live that purpose, and take action in creating a life where you can ruthlessly pursue that thing. Fail along the way, bounce back, and keep going. The one thing stopping you from achieving that magical moment of passion, purpose, and profession all living together is taking *action!*

TL;DR

No matter where we live on the ask continuum (from an askhole to someone who lets asks pass them by), we must start moving into the direction of taking action (or sometimes saving our asks a bit longer). Double down on connection and then go in for the ask.

Make the Connection

- The right time in a relationship to go for the ask is 10 percent after you think you need it more than life itself, according to super-connector Bogdan Constantin. Find one ask you want to make and figure out when to do it.
- Understand your sales cycle. Learn to recognize where people are in the sales cycle. Build rapport and add value while they move along the sales cycle. And ask when people are getting close to the end of the sales cycle.
- Go ahead and get a couple of rejections out of the way, then take action on developing some of your biggest sales leads or networking prospects. Identify three and write them on your whiteboard or mirror.

CHAPTER 10:

How to Go for the Ask

Nathalie Molina Niño, author of *Leapfrog: The New Revolution for Women Entrepreneurs*, is furious with me.

Fortunately, she lives nearly 1,000 miles away from me in New York City, where she works as a builder capitalist at Outcomes Over Optics and advises high-growth tech companies around the globe that benefit women and the planet. She's a force.

But she and I disagree a bit about life being a ruthless pursuit of passion.

"I come from a family that immigrated here and worked in the sweatshops of L.A.," she confessed to me. "I guarantee you my family was not passionate about working 15-hour days in a factory in downtown L.A."

Nathalie believes that the majority of people are just focused on keeping a roof over their heads, especially in a country where most people don't have enough savings to cover two weeks of living expenses. She rightfully pointed out to me that it can seem dangerous and privileged to believe everything will magically work out if you simply follow your passion.

This isn't what we disagree about. I agree that her family (and others) aren't likely to be passionate about working double shifts in factories. I also agree that it can seem privileged to believe everything will "magically" work out if you simply follow your passion.

What I disagree with Nathalie about is her opinion that your day job needs to directly revolve around your passion. Of course, it's much more pleasant if that's the case. But day jobs are just one way to chase your passions. Many people love their lives by pursuing their passions outside of work hours through side hustles, home time, or hobbies. As long as their day job is an overall positive experience, many people live completely fulfilling lives even if their day job doesn't directly reflect their passions.

That's where our disagreement ends, however. For example, Nathalie also agrees that people could be passionate about what their day job makes possible for them, even if it doesn't directly represent their big passions. "The fact is, while my parents might not have been passionate about sewing clothing in a factory," she explains, "what they *were* passionate about was the byproduct of that, which was being about to pull their family out of poverty into owning our first home and sending their kids to college—*that* was their passion."

This doesn't undermine the idea of pursuing passions, Nathalie says. She just suggests that people generally focus their "ruthless pursuits" on solving real problems, not on chasing their passions. "This is a really great equation for starting a business or setting your North Star for your career—solving real problems. And, chances are, if you do focus your efforts on starting a business or setting your North Star to solve real problems in your life or in other people's lives, you'll likely end up doing something you can be passionate about."

And *this* is where Nathalie and I *completely* agree. We view passion from a different angle—me as the primary driver and her as the byproduct of "solving real problems"—but, in practice, if you focus on solving real problems, you'll be much more successful if you focus on solving a problem you care about solving. That sounds a lot like pursuing something you're passionate about to me.

This chapter is dedicated to making your asks last no matter where your passions or your problem-solving skills lie. We'll discuss the new economy of giving, some time-tested advice on genuine connections, and a way to remove those tacking "Hello, My Name Is …" stickers once and for all.

Race to the Middle

Baby goats. Sometimes, all you need to make a genuine connection for life are a few baby goats. This is what I discovered when I was at a dinner with some potential clients, and after the initial excitement of getting to know each other, things simmered down. I was nervous. I really wanted to make an impression on one person in particular, whom we'll call Len.

For a moment, it seemed we'd run out of things to talk about. Then, somehow, the discussion got around to baby goats. Len nearly choked on his steak as his eyes grew wide. "I love baby goats!" he exclaimed, gushing about how he'd just adopted two baby goats. "I'm going to be dead serious with you guys," he said. "These goats have brought me more joy than anything else in the last year." And for the next 20 minutes, we talked about baby goats. That was it—that was all it took to establish a real relationship with Len. A few months later, I ran into him in the Salt Lake City airport. He said, "Hey, it's the Millennial Whisperer!" and I said right back, "Hey, it's the Goat Whisperer!"

My dinner with Len is just one example of the race to the middle when you're trying to find the common connection point that will make you unforgettable. Len and I now catch up every couple of months, and I'm helping him discover his next chapter, which would have never happened had I not pointed out that the only thing in his life that lit him up was baby goats. Len and I have not had any business transactions yet, but I can almost guarantee you that a byproduct of this connection will be us doing business together.

Finding a common connection point can be easier than you think. Rory Cooper points out the nature of networking in Washington, D.C. "Everybody here is from somewhere else, so you can start with, 'Where are you from?' And that usually gives you a pretty quick roadmap to how you can connect with the person. For me, I've been to 48 states, so I know most areas of this country. I can relate to most places and say: 'I've got friends there,' or 'I went to school there,' or 'I spent a week there doing this.' People want to talk about their homes, especially here where they don't live where they grew up. Being able to get people to be able to open up about growing up and where they're from is a good way to start navigating that road. The joke in Washington is that everybody starts every conversation with 'What do you do?' but I start every conversation with 'Where you from?'"

"When you create unique moments and experiences, it more times than not opens the door to create a more unique and bidirectional connection. If you are willing to go deeper with that person or that moment, you will no doubt create a more memorable and lasting impression." —**Cary Franklin**

Ken Hannaman, the Northeast Division Vice President of Arby's, always asks people about their personal goals as a conversation starter when he's in restaurants and talking about driving the business and giving the best guest experience possible. "I love talking to people," he says. "It could be a general manager; it could be an assistant manager, a shift manager, or a team member who's making $9 an hour. I usually ask them what they're working on, and then I ask, 'What are some things that you're passionate about in life? Where do you see yourself going?'"

Those conversations, says Ken, usually lead into other connection points. "It starts with finding ways for me to help connect people to where their goals and aspirations may take them. And then a lot of times they'll ask me about the paths I've taken. I don't always have all the answers that they seek. But when you go into those kinds of conversations with a true purpose and meaning, and you're not trying to get anything personally out of it, life seems to pay you back ten-fold."

Dan Scalia says that 95 percent of his networking conversations are surface level; breaking through to the 5 percent leading to a tremendous amount of value requires diving deeper. "You can only get to that point by being super vulnerable," he says.

You can also use this tactic to turn a bad interaction into a positive one. On my first big trip to Nike, I had to leave the hotel super early in the morning to set up my presentation. When my Uber arrived at 5 a.m., I rushed into his brand-new red Toyota Camry. In my haste to get in the car with my business partner, Tyler, I apparently closed the door a bit too hard. The driver immediately yelled back at us: "*This car is brand new!* How about treating it with a little *respect?!*" Tyler then whispered into my ear, "This is going to be a looong trip to Nike."

I was determined to turn the negative first impression into a positive, though, and knew the race to the middle would give me a perfect opportunity to do so. Of course, I started by letting him know that I didn't mean to slam it that hard, which he appreciated. But I then immediately shifted to asking the driver about his accent, which I recognized as a Caribbean accent. He told me he was from Trinidad and Tobago, which got us talking about how I *love* the steel drum music from his island and how much I wanted to visit there to go kiteboarding. By the end of the 30-minute drive, he had invited me to visit his family's place there to go kiteboarding and we exchanged contact info. I had successfully turned an uncomfortable situation into a positive connection.

Mask Your Ask in Your Dream

When you tell people what your dream is, they will do everything in their power to help you achieve it.

My friend Corey Hackett has a dream to bring more confidence to men through, among other things, image consulting. He's pursuing this dream while he works for a custom suit design company called Blank Label. He recently sold me a tux, told me about his dream, and asked who in my network he needed to meet to help make this dream come true. He masked an ask for a connection within a big dream of helping bring more confidence to men. This is a perfect example of a simple ask masked in a dream. I immediately started thinking of potential connections to make.

I apply this to the incredible meetings I've been able to have while writing *Save Your Asks*, too. I say, "It is my dream to create a handbook, to create *the* handbook, for making people better networkers and sellers while also helping them live more fulfilling and purpose-filled lives. Who in your network do I have to talk to?"

When we mask our asks in our dreams, people can sense a more genuine purpose in your ask. They can see that you're not just trying to make more money. And they are much more willing to open doors for you. And suddenly, you see your network quickly increase from all your new introduction. Mask your ask in your dream and go to your strongest advocates. You have to be selling yourself in every single conversation so the more people who understand what your dream is, the more likely it will come true. Remember, this dream must be *authentic*! If you start masking your ask in a fake dream, this will have the opposite effect— people will just dismiss you.

Ask for Advice First

Remember Quincy Jones, the super-connector we met in chapter 1? Quincy taught me one of the greatest networking and relationship-building tactics I've ever learned: asking for personal advice first. He has built one of the most impressive networks I've ever seen. I asked him how he created such amazing relationships. He answered, "Chris, I love asking for *personal* advice first because it automatically gets us to a place of vulnerability. Asking for personal advice causes the other person to think more deeply than by asking for a business or networking tip. It causes them to share something deeper within their head and heart that will help you as a human being."

When Quincy meets someone, he'll have researched their background so extensively that asking for personal advice feels natural. Then he can expand into the head and the heart of genuine connection.

Sneaky? No. He is genuinely asking for personal advice to help him grow in an area his contact has excelled. This is human connection at its best, which gets completely lost in the pace of today's professional and even personal world: sharing common advice and experience to help others improve in areas that matter most to them.

Recently, I was researching a connection before one of my meetings and discovered that the person had spoken openly about his struggle with dyslexia. My daughter Finley had just been diagnosed with dyslexia, so it was a natural connection point as I asked him about books, schools, and other resources to help me. He shared incredible advice with me, and we built a deeper bond than the typical "networking" meeting.

Be Specific

When I asked Dave Heath, the founder of Bombas sock company, for the best piece of advice about saving your asks, he immediately responded that people should be much more specific in their asks.

"It's easier for those in positions of either helping you or mentoring you because typically the people you're going to ask are busy," says Dave. "I've had a lot of mentors carve time out of their days to speak with me and guide me along the way. I was very pointed to say, 'Hey, could you help me answer this very specific question?'"

Dave's not alone either. Virtually every successful person will give you similar advice. "Whenever somebody reaches out, if they can convey a high degree of authenticity and purpose, those are the people who I end up saying, 'I'm happy to take a phone call with you,'" says Dan Scalia. "But the best advice I can give is to be more specific with your ask."

Everyone's got those super-connectors within their networks. Identify who you want to meet and then work backward, finding their connections with friends or colleagues in your own network. As super-connector Aaron Abrahms told me, people will want to help you as much as they can—provided you're passionate and specific about your vision.

As an advertising executive, for example, I'm trying to meet with CMOs, so in my networking conversations I ask, "Hey, do you know anyone who's a CMO?" Add another layer by orienting your questions around your dream. I might mask my ask in my dream by saying, "It is my dream to have a greater impact on the world, specifically through the advertising work we do. I'm trying to meet with CMOs of large Consumer Packaged Goods, or CPG, companies or in the insurance vertical; is there anyone in your network you feel like I could benefit from meeting?"

One disclaimer that I must add here: *Make sure you are being authentic.* This cannot be something that you fake in order to get to the next meeting. You must feel this within your soul! When I tell people about my dream to have a greater impact on the world, they can feel it. It doesn't matter if I'm on the phone, on Zoom, or face-to-face. You know I mean it.

Shawshank. Shawshank. And Shawshank Some More.

Shawshanking. It's a thing, and it's my favorite verb in this new world of networking. Since the movie *The Shawshank Redemption* was released, fans have ascribed a few different meanings to the term, but my favorite is this: "To slowly chip away at getting to know someone in order to get into a relationship with them, in the way Tim Robbins' character slowly chips away at his prison cell to eventually break out of jail in the movie."[18]

If you remember from the movie, Tim Robbins' character wrote several letters to the prison authority asking for funds to

---

18   SlangDefine.org, "Slang Define: What Is Shawshanking? - Meaning and Definition," in *Slangdefine.org,* accessed June 25, 2021, https://slangdefine. org/s/shawshanking-72f4.html.

outfit a new library. Every week for two years, he mailed these letters, with no response until he finally received a check for $200. But he didn't stop there—he kept writing until, 10 years later, Shawshank had the nicest library in the prison system. That character, Andy Dufresne, is one of the most memorable movie characters I've seen, and his methodical work pays off.

My first experience with shawshanking came from being on the receiving end of Jason Beckerman's shawshanking. I had signed a huge technology deal with Jason, a serial entrepreneur from New York. We had known each other for seven years but had never done business together. After we closed the deal, I asked Jason about his business and how he managed to keep focused for seven years. "I get easily distracted," I noted. "How did you keep going for seven years without knowing if we'd ever do business together?"

His response changed the way I looked at networking forever: "Easy. I shawshanked you." The blank look on my face likely said everything I needed to, so he continued. "Every single week for the last seven years, I've had a touchpoint with you. Some weeks it's been through Facebook Messenger. Others, it's been on Instagram, text, or email. But every single week I've made a touchpoint with you, and now here we are. Basically, I chip-, chip-, chipped away until the right opportunity presented itself to do business together. A letter a week. I shawshanked you."

I had just gotten a call from the CMO of a Fortune 50 company. She wanted to hire me as their next head of internet marketing and social media. I had no interest in the position, but I *did* want that company to hire my agency. *Maybe I could shawshank her*, I thought. Over time, that could lead to even bigger and better opportunities for everyone. I decided to switch my approach and try my hands at shawshanking, so I called her, told her I wasn't open to leaving my agency but offered to help her find the right person. We connected every week and not once did I ask her to hire my agency. I was just being helpful. Eighteen months later, she hired my agency for our first projects. Now, they're one of our largest clients with more than 60 people dedicated to that account. And it all started with shawshanking.

Importantly, not once during that shawshank period did I go in for an ask. I was set on doing the "give" first and developing a genuine connection and relationship throughout it before asking for anything. The relationship was important enough to wait. Sure enough, the head of marketing at that Fortune 50 company became one of my close friends, and my agency earned an enormous client.

And that's how most of my stories go—these "prospects" end up becoming good friends of mine—because I aim for friendship even though the people are prospects for my agency. People will ask me if, during shawshanking someone, what happens if you don't like them? That's easy: You don't want them as clients because it will be short-lived and miserable. Focus on prospects and shawshanking with *good* people, where it doesn't feel forced.

Shawshanking can take other forms as well. Remember Randy Smith? If you ask Randy about how he got his first break, he'll tell you how he brought donuts to Pulte Homes headquarters in south Florida every week for more than a year. One Friday afternoon, his tenacity finally paid off. Their other flooring contractor had dropped the ball and a new decision-maker had just taken over. Sure enough, they allowed Randy to make a bid that became his big break. Pulte Homes became his tentpole account, allowing him to grow.

Turn Your "Let's" Into "By When?"

As a vice president at GoDaddy, Geoff Clawson has learned plenty of networking tools, but perhaps none so timeless as the act of actually scheduling instead of resorting to that nebulous phrase of "Let's have coffee sometime," or "Let's meet up next week." Geoff was in junior high when the original Tony Robbins cassette tapes were released, and he listened to a set his mom had been given. As a seventh grader, some of the material went right over his head. "But one of the things that I totally got immediately because I was already pretty goal-oriented," he says, "is that if you don't schedule it, it will never happen. So you can say 'Let's' all you want. But it's the 'By when?' that makes it actionable and relevant."

When Geoff was working at Facebook, I told him we'd move a big chunk of my ad agency's budget to Facebook. "Let's do it," I said. He immediately responded, "By when?" Geoff then explained the importance of accountability with statements like "let's." It made a huge impression on me—six months later, my agency had not only made the Facebook spend but also was having incredible results. By sticking to a deadline, I'd created my own success through connecting with Geoff. We've all had countless experiences of hearing someone say, "Let's grab a drink or coffee" or "Let's do dinner with our spouses." Then *nothing* happens. Instead, respond with a "By when?"

One afternoon, I was at my daughter's soccer game and began talking with my neighbor Neil, who I didn't really know well at the time. I'd seen him walking in the neighborhood, and as we watched the game, I mentioned how he looked much stronger. He said he'd been working with this amazing personal trainer, Tramell Smith.

I said, "Let's work out together ..." and then caught myself. "By when can we do that?"

"Monday at 5 a.m."

Since that day, I've worked out with Neil and Tramell three mornings a week at Pinnacle Fitness, and I've put on about 25 pounds of muscle and am in the best shape of my life at 40. This is also the same Neil who got me one of my first huge speaking engagements at Cox Enterprises when he was an executive there. The story continues: I then helped introduce Neil to my friend Hank McLarty (remember Hank from my mastermind the Great Eight?). Now, as I write, Neil has been the president of Gratus Capital for more than a year, and our families are best friends. This is how networking—*connecting*—works. Connection comes with accountability and time!

The important part here is also *action*. So many people in today's world fail to walk the talk, and there's a massive void for accountability. Take your next "networking" event that you attend. How many times will someone say, "Let's grab a coffee to talk more" or "Let's do dinner to connect further" and then *nothing* happens? I *challenge* you to answer any "Let's" with a "By when?" and watch how fast something real materializes because one of two things will happen: Either you'll find yourself connecting with that individual over Zoom, at coffee, or over dinner. Or you'll quickly discover this was an empty ask and that person doesn't really want to connect with you and was just saying it to be cordial.

Create Memorable Experiences

It was a dream come true for any golf fan—or anybody, really—VIP passes to the Masters Tournament at Augusta, Georgia. And it just so happened that friends were in town to entertain big clients and high-value sales prospects. I called Quincy Jones and asked if he'd gotten a limo for all of us to the Masters event.

Quincy said no; there was no limo. "Meet me at Peachtree Dekalb Airport," he said. "We're taking two helicopters instead."

After an incredible time at the tournament, we took the helicopters back to Atlanta, flying over the factories, fields, and farms of Georgia. Late afternoon thunderstorms were popping up in the distance, and our pilot expertly dodged them. "Buzz the fields!" Quincy exclaimed over his headset to the pilot, asking him to dip down closer to the fields below. After about the 23rd request, the pilot finally plunged the helicopter to hover 100 feet above the fields in the middle of Georgia. Our friends and clients were blown away. It was exhilarating—and a shared experience for everyone aboard. I mean we could have just *gone* to the Masters, but Quincy knew we had to take it to the next level.

Now, Quincy and I call it "buzzing the fields"—creating experiences that people will remember forever. Instead of shuffling through a networking event, it's taking it to the next level (literally, in this case) to put a new price on the power of connection. Whether I'm hitting the singletrack with the CMO of Specialized or bringing a new client to experience Umi, I'm always brainstorming ways to invest in a shared experience that will garner way more "wows" than generic, meaningless gestures. Think about how many times everyone who took those helicopters has talked about it to friends and family.

Find the Meaning

Since founding the Sprinkles cupcake company I discussed in chapter 2, Candace Nelson has become one of the country's top food celebrities, appearing regularly on *Cupcake Wars* and *Sugar Rush*. She and her husband, Charles, have now pivoted again to create CN2 Ventures, investing in early-stage and growth-stage companies, including Pizzana and Play2Progress. She's a natural target for newbie networkers who have yet to learn how to save their asks.

"I'll get people who DM me on Instagram: 'Hey, love your work, you're great, would love to collab with you,'" says Candace. "I'm up for working with people. But I would like some more specifics: 'Who are you? What specifically do you have in mind?' It's gotten a little too casual. Sometimes it's so flippant, it feels rude and presumptuous."

So what does work for getting the attention of people like Candace Nelson? Respect for people's time, she says. "Researching me more is really helpful. People don't do their homework. Show that you care, which plays into the idea of respect. Also, a well-crafted email really goes a long way." Do your research and make specific, meaningful asks!

When Lydia Fenet was writing *The Most Powerful Woman in the Room Is You*, she asked other powerful women to write their stories of negotiation, connection, and confidence. It was just a plain ask—no time for shawshanking, race to the middle, or some of the other techniques in this book—an ask for a paragraph or two, 150 words, on their own experiences in becoming powerful. While she already knew such contributors as Martha Stewart and Arianna Huffington, she needed women to share their stories and emailed her good friends with connections in different worlds.

Half of those people ended up in the book. So 50 percent of them rejected Lydia's request. "But 50 percent said yes!" she says. By processing those rejections early on with an abundance mindset, Lydia was able to find even more confidence, not only in writing *The Most Powerful Woman in the Room Is You*, but also in her career at Christie's and her newly expanded network. Plus, she could include advice like this from Alexandra Lebenthal, who *Fortune* named "The Queen of Wall Street":

"A lot of people think that networking is about going to events and meeting people, but it is really about cultivating a group of people who can be instrumental to you, and, equally important, you to them. When I meet someone and we have any kind of meaningful conversation, they go into my physical contacts, but also into my mental Rolodex. I begin a gradual process of getting to know them. If I see good news about someone or their organization, I will send a short email. I also reach out to people when there is news that may not be positive. People appreciate those emails and calls more than the congratulatory ones. Figure out how you can connect people you know with one another in ways that are beneficial to them. Find ways to do that, like having a lunch or dinner for a group of people. There are some important rules to remember when networking. The second contact you have with someone should not be to ask for something. That is a way to immediately turn someone off. Also, there may be times when someone does not respond to your efforts to connect with them. Don't push it. Just move on to those who will."[19]

Jeff Raider, the founder of Warby Parker and Harry's razors, finds energy in making meaningful connections. He shared with me how he engages with walking meetings. "Now, more than ever, it's important to spend time checking in with people, really trying to understand what's going on in their lives and how that's impacting their work," he says, relaying a recent walking meeting in which he discovered how a team member was going through the time-consuming process of moving apartments in New York. "Understanding what's going on with other people enables you to empathize in a completely different way." Jeff has successfully built two billion-dollar enterprises with connection at the core of both.

---

19 Lydia Fenet, *The Most Powerful Woman in the Room Is You: Command an Audience and Sell Your Way to Success* (New York: Gallery Books, 2019), Kindle.

This starts with your people and then should also manifest into how you approach customers.

Create "Everybody Wins" Connections

One of the best ways to build relationships with people is to help them become successful. For example, when Giovanni "Gio" Di Palma, the owner of Antico Pizza Napoletana, became one of the millions of entrepreneurs hit hard by COVID-19, Quincy Jones suggested he send some frozen pies to a handful of influential people. His frozen pizzas are some of the best in the world, and Quincy knew his efforts would earn him some low-cost attention and potentially a few new customers.

One of the people Gio sent pizzas to was Dave Portnoy, the president of Barstool Sports, who is known for his video pizza reviews, which are viewed millions of times by Portnoy's ultraloyal following. Sure enough, Portnoy reviewed the pizza, giving it one of the highest ratings ever, and Gio sold more than 5,000 pies as a result. Gio's business was back, all because of some creative problem-solving through gift giving.

When Hank McLarty heard about what Gio had done, he decided to do something similar with Gio's pizzas. When it became clear that COVID-19 would keep us cooped up for some time, Hank decided to do something special for his wealth management clients to benefit Gio too. As the CEO of Gratus Capital, he prides himself on always putting his clients' needs first. In this case, however, Hank knew that his clients were natural givers. So he decided to gift his clients Antico Pizza Napoletana to donate to anyone they wanted. His clients were high-net-worth families and didn't need the pizzas. But because they were all givers, he decided to take a deeper approach to giving, while helping Gio and Gio's employees in the process. See how amazing the world of genuine connections can be?

In this case, everyone won. Gio's sales skyrocketed when he got such a favorable review from Dave Portnoy and Hank's order. Hank got to build deeper relationships with his wealth management clients. Dave Portnoy got more content for his popular pizza review series (and an amazing pizza). And Quincy got to build deeper connections with everyone, as super-connectors often do.

Send (Only) Meaningful Gifts

If you are already spending money on client or prospect gifts, you might be able to save some money and make much better connections by buying fewer, but better gifts.

Type "networking gifts" into the Google search box and chances are you'll find something along the lines I did: "18 Cheap Thank You Gifts for Your Career Network" from a site called The Muse and "20 Low Cost Networking Gifts" from the Shepa Learning Company. Another site promises boxes of cigars among "corporate gifts they'll remember" while Etsy offers doormats and mugs labeled "the CEO" among its networking gift selection.

Yikes! Cheap and low cost? No thank you. Really, that's a *no* for thank-you gifts to anyone new (or old) in your network. If I got a doormat, I'd probably slam the door in your face, and a mug, no matter how personalized, is probably the least personal gift ever.

Delivering just the right present takes more talent and time than simply going online, as John Ruhlin explains in *Giftology: The Art and Science of Using Gifts to Cut Through the Noise, Increase Referrals, and Strengthen Retention*.[20]

---

20 John Ruhlin, *Giftology: The Art and Science of Using Gifts to Cut through the Noise, Increase Referrals, and Strengthen Retention* (Lioncrest Publishing, 2016).

"Gift giving and those 'little touches' commemorate not just certain events, but people, places, and things that are important to us," he writes. "In essence, they become the symbols of the value you place on the relationship. Go back into our deepest history, and you'll see it—even during biblical times. As social beings, gift giving has remained near universal for people, regardless of their origin."

Ruhlin writes of creating a "first-class experience," from treating people to a night at the Ritz-Carlton to spending $1,500 on a dinner. He also cites this example of giftology:

"A few years ago, I was in Vegas for a business conference that featured top executives from major companies all over the world. I met up with a group of entrepreneurs who were former Fortune 500 executives. They had identified an elite group of people they needed to connect with in order to get their businesses off the ground or to the next level. High on their list was the president of Target's electronic division, a very large multibillion-dollar part of Target's business. For eighteen months, they had tried everything they could think of to get a meeting with this guy—and for eighteen months the only response they got was silence. I knew we had to do something big and bold that would just blow him away, so we did some research and discovered he was a graduate of the University of Minnesota. We then hired a custom furniture company to have the Minnesota Gopher logo and fight song carved into a fifty-inch long, sixty-pound piece of cherry wood. Within twenty-four hours, his assistant called.

"I don't know who you are, and he's completely booked this week," she began, "but next Tuesday at 3 p.m., you have 30 minutes to talk about whatever it is that you want to talk about."

At the end of the day, however, giftology is not about manipulating people through lavish spending. It's not just about standing out by being different. It's about taking the time to understand what will make an impact, no matter how large or small. It can be as simple as making someone smile. Instead of "low cost" or "cheap" or extravagant and expensive, think in terms of what brings you a little joy in your life.

"When you stay at a nice hotel, you appreciate when the janitor, front-desk clerk, or cleaning lady smiles and says, 'Good morning,'" writes Ruhlin. "It makes a world of difference with your overall experience when you're shown that a company believes in the importance of small touches ... These are the small things that people notice and remember as big things ... Giftology gives you the power to make people feel over the moon about your relationship with them, no matter who they are."

Focus on Sustaining Relationships

"You can't sustain every relationship, but you learn the ones that are meaningful do sustain."
—Rory Cooper

The simplest way to figure out if someone should be in your network is to ask yourself the question, "Is this person someone I want to hang out with?" If you don't like a person, you don't want them as a client, so don't go chasing them. You need that genuine connection we've discussed. I connect with people who are like-minded, who I want to be friends with, and who I trust.

Every single one of my networking stories ends up the same way: these people end up becoming buddies, or even some of my best friends.

"Networking is all about our survival," says Jasen Trautwein. "When someone reveals their authenticity to us, it's a heart connection. Your heart radiates energy waves. And when you connect with someone, it affects their heart and their chemistry. They're getting more oxytocin and serotonin. That's how lifetime bonds are made."

In a 2020 article for the *Harvard Business Review*,[21] Rosabeth Moss Kanter explains how individuals can help solve big social problems through the power of connection. In "Networking Doesn't Have to Be Self-Serving," she shares six essential lessons from successful leaders who have used their currency-brokering skills in small ways to make big changes:

1. Show up.
2. Knock on many doors.
3. Help your way into inner circles.
4. Ask to be taught.
5. Plant seeds and pre-sell.
6. Demonstrate and deliver.

Like any relationship, maintaining meaningful connections takes continual work. It never ends. Would you stop listening to your best friend or taking your kids to events they enjoy or calling your mom on her birthday? The same goes for business relationships, only on the terms you've established. If you initially connected over a common interest in Swedish DJs, then reach out every once in a while to share a song on Spotify. If you get a laugh out of their Instagram posts, message them. Or if you can't figure out why you continue to think about what a terrible bore this person was, then let it go.

---

21 Rosabeth Moss Kanter, "Networking Doesn't Have to Be Self-Serving," *Harvard Business Review*, March 6, 2020, https://hbr.org/2020/03/networking-doesnt-have-to-be-self-serving.

"You create this at the beginning—you create a relationship," says Rory Cooper. "You have an informational meeting, or you meet at a reception or over coffee or lunch, and you figure out what you two want to do for each other—what the relationship kind of feels like. The people you're really going to connect and engage with are those who have a positive role in your life, or vice versa. You'll keep finding meaningful ways to engage with each other. And other people will fall away once you've had your moment in time. I still have very close relationships with interns I had 15 years ago, and then I've got interns from two years ago who I'll probably never speak to again. And it's not that one person necessarily was better than the other. It's just that the person from 15 years ago managed to create a more meaningful relationship where I'm more invested in them and they feel more invested in me."

Successfully sustaining good relationships means

- Communication
- Vulnerability
- Reciprocity without scorekeeping
- Staying in tune with their life changes, personally and professionally

When someone comes to mind, I immediately text them as I've discovered there's a good reason I've been thinking of them, whether it's because they can connect me with a sales lead, or because they can be a good connection for someone else in my network. I also tee-up future experiences for my business relationships, listening to their interests, and taking advantage of the time I have to track down VIP tickets or make a hard-to-get restaurant reservation. I'm also constantly writing down observations and to-dos in my (Nike Volt Yellow, of course) notebook. Just the other day I texted a prospect who had moved to Hawaii as I was watching *The White Lotus* on HBO. He immediately texted back that we needed to catch up because he had a project that he wanted my agency to work on for him. Boom, it works!

TL;DR

The worst thing you can do is to continue doing things the same way you've been doing them. Just do *something* to help create more connection and more momentum in your life as it relates to your network. Shawshank away with a few key relationships and just watch what happens!

Make the Connection

- Make your asks last by orienting them around something more meaningful.
- Schedule your next meeting to be something more exciting and memorable than coffee.
- Practice a "race to the middle" in your next social outing and see how long it takes you to find common ground. You can even start timing yourself for how long it takes.
- Send a gift or thank-you note to someone who has helped you out recently.
- Look at your list of sales and networking prospects and rank them from "most likely to hang out with socially" to least likely. This will determine where you should prioritize your efforts.
- Connection takes time—use tools such as social media to deepen your connections. Commit to at least one tool to help you achieve this.
- Do copious research (as if you're going to interview them for a podcast) before reaching out to a prospect. Find one prospect and put in at least one hour of research before

reaching out to them. See how much more effective this can be.

- Progress is happiness. Make sure you're always moving forward, cultivating your passions alongside your currency. Do three small things today to help you move forward and create momentum.

- Send a text or video message to someone you haven't had a touchpoint with in the last three months.

CHAPTER 11:

The Connection Economy

Before you go into the world saving your asks and building authentic connections, I want to tie together all the tips, stories, and strategies into two simple principles for you.

First, we live in a connection economy in which our connections will determine our economics. In other words, your future will depend more on your connections than on your talents. The more and better connections you build, the better your future will become. And when you build authentic connections based on your true passions, you can easily achieve that wonderful world where your passion, purpose, and profession collide.

Second, when going in for the ask, subtle shifts can make a big difference. In the last chapter, I shared several strategies and principles for making true, authentic asks. In this chapter, I want to focus on some of the more frequently used methods of communication and outreach people use (for better or worse) to attempt to build connection in our digital world. There truly is a hierarchy of connection, and it doesn't matter how eloquent you are, if you are constantly using shallow, impersonal methods of connection, you'll build shallow, transactional relationships.

So although I could have discussed the connection economy and hierarchy of connection in chapter 10, they deserve their own chapter. Keep both of these concepts close to mind (and heart) as you take action and make connections and you can become more successful than you ever thought possible.

The Connection Economy

It's all about connecting the dots. In the galaxy of opportunity that our entrepreneurial world is today, we just need to see how those pinpoints of light work together. The premise is simple: Create the connection first, and then go in with the give. Save your asks, resonate with good energy, and the reciprocity will come—even if it takes a few months or a year.

That's what makes super-connectors a little different—they get a huge high from helping others and connecting with others. You can feel the energy. When I interviewed Karissa Kouchis (Tony Robbins' right-hand woman), for example, she said that when you show up at any meeting, you've got to bring good energy. You can't show up with low-a** energy. "LAE," she calls it. If you find your energy is consistently low in your meetings with people, maybe you're approaching it the wrong way!

"Think about networking as another form of energy. Whether you're exchanging names or information, what you are actually exchanging is energy." —**Shelley Paxton**

Experts back us up on this. As a 2020 *Forbes* article explains, reciprocity, relationships, and resonance are fueling a different way of doing business.[22]

"The connection economy is the economy of prosperity, collaboration and infinite possibilities," writes Peace Mitchell. "It's the vision of an economic ecosystem, a complex network of interconnected systems built on trust, value alignment and reciprocity.

"As society continues to evolve beyond the industrial economy and the information economy, we are seeing personal connection, trust and authentic relationships emerge to become valuable commodities. This economy is significantly different from those that came before because inherent in this economy is the connection to a deeper sense of community, purpose and meaning over mass production, competition and consumption."

Super-connectors are powerful because connection is great for business. As marketing becomes noisier, standing out from the crowd is vital, and the best way to stand out is to develop a relationship with your audience. Forming clever, strategic collaborations with businesses that are complementary to yours has the power to open the doors to new opportunities, customers, and profits.

The Hierarchy of Connection

When it comes to the longer sales cycles most of us are following, we can engage with someone we don't know in so many ways, thanks to the spectrum of connection many fail to realize.

Here's what each of these looks like, starting from the far left in this hierarchy of connection.

---

22   Peace Mitchell, "The Connection Economy: Using Resonance, Reciprocity and Relationships for Networking," *Forbes*, October 13, 2020, https://www.forbes.com/sites/forbesbusinesscouncil/2020/10/13/the-connection-economy-using-resonance-reciprocity-and-relationships-for-networking/?sh=76bb76cc615e.

The Blanketed Email or LinkedIn Message

Using automation or bots, you send hundreds of messages to prospects who live within certain parameters. You either buy email addresses or pay for InMail messages with the hopes that a small percentage actually reply to your request. Oftentimes, these have links to case studies or research that the salesperson just expects the prospect to click on or open: "Would you have 15 minutes to hop on a Zoom or call with me?" Um, *no!* You may *think* this is working for you as you are playing the numbers game, but more than likely, you are just checking the box to feel productive.

The harsh reality is, you are alienating and even pissing off your highest value potential customers! This may be a good strategy for short sales cycles, cheap products, or software offerings, but it's definitely not the best approach for the longer sales cycle of six-plus weeks and any products or services worth more than a couple hundred dollars a month. There are few exceptions to this, especially on LinkedIn. One of these exceptions is my friend Andrew Frank, who has created a company called Accelerain. He suggests making your LinkedIn requests super short and write them like you're already a friend of theirs (don't be super formal). Instead of saying what you're selling, just focus on the connection. Once the connection is accepted, wait two to three months before you go in for an ask and try to develop that relationship over the two to three months.

The Blanketed Call

You get the phone numbers of your prospects. You call a few times and leave a message, hoping they'll call you back. Think about how you use your phone. Do you pick up unknown numbers? What makes you think a CEO or other executive would?

At this point, you're just one step above a robocaller. I once had a guy named Ryan call me from eight different numbers. I made the mistake of finally answering one of his calls because I thought it was my daughter's school. Instead of making a genuine connection, he had harassed me until he finally tricked me into answering his call. When I realized what was going on, I quickly ended the call by saying, "Please remove me from your list!" (We'll talk more about these strategies soon. Also, Ryan, I hope you're reading this because you were not only wasting your ask you were also ruining your reputation, one blanketed call at a time.)

The Message with a Common Connection While Providing Little Insight or Value

This is the email or message you send that's just one step better than asking for someone to hop on a call. These emails usually ask some sort of generic question about their company's audience or frustrations, and you provide some sort of case study or link out to a study that you find groundbreaking but that most prospects just ignore. These emails almost never work.

The Message with a Little Bit of Research

Now we're getting somewhere. This is where you do a bit of research not just on the prospect's company but also on that person specifically. The more robust your research and understanding that you can convey in that message, the more likely you are to work your way toward a real meeting. I recently responded to a guy named Blake who had sent me four worthless emails. I finally said, "Why not do a bit of research before reaching out?" He responded that if he researched everyone he was reaching out to, he wouldn't be able to hit his prospecting numbers. I told him "That's okay, cut your prospecting numbers by 80 percent and

192 | **SAVE YOUR ASKS**

watch how much more effective you can be with the remaining 20 percent."

The Warm Intro from a Common Connection
(Who Is Actually an Advocate)

Ideally, this would be from someone who *has actually worked with you or used your company*. I have people reach out to me all the time asking for an introduction to a high-level executive: "Chris, I see you are connected to John Smith on LinkedIn; can you introduce us?" Many times this comes from someone that I have not done business with in the past. And they usually have no idea about my relationship with John Smith. What a waste of an ask.

Instead, we must be *selective* about where we focus introductions and limit them to those for whom we're truly an advocate. When we do this effectively, it can be massively successful. This is also an opportunity for "masking your ask in your dream."

A much better approach would be for this person to ask a mentor to help make the connection. The mentor might write: "Chris, we met at the Audi dealership last year. My friend Alyssa is hoping to meet with John Smith about a job, and she is an incredible salesperson. Could you make an introduction between the two of them?"

The In-Person "Race to the Middle"

You did it! You finally got in the same conference or Zoom room as your prospects. Ideally, you arrive having done some research on who is in the room so as you navigate it, you can create some shortcuts toward your "race to the middle." These can be very impactful interactions, and you'll want to end your conversation with your prospect by turning your "let's" into "by when."

You say, "Let's grab coffee so I can take you through some work we've done in your space." They respond with "Great!" You then ask, "By when would you like to meet?" and take out your phone to schedule a date. It's at this moment things move from an early-stage prospect into a real prospect.

The Connection Catalyst

Being the connection catalyst is a great way to hit a group of prospects together while offering up a "give" vs. an "ask." It's where you bring people together and offer some sort of value, which can just be allowing them to meet and talk to one another over cocktails (remember Aaron Abrahms?)

Don't overthink this. I was recently asked to speak for an insurance benefits company about *The Millennial Whisperer* and a few hundred HR people showed up to hear my speech and get a free book with a signed nameplate from me and the benefits company. This created both reciprocity and new touchpoints with potential clients for the benefits company!

The In-Person Warm Introduction

There is almost no better introduction than when someone in your network is willing to introduce you to a prospect in person *with* you. This can be incredibly effective as it helps break the ice with them, and it makes the prospect feel comfortable out of the gates.

Sometimes you will meet with the prospect after a warm introduction without them attending (which is fine), but when it's the three of you, magic happens. You're essentially able to leverage their relationship with each other to create an opportunity. Also remember, no one can sell you as well as an advocate via an in-person referral.

The Shared Experience

Sometimes it's hard for us to break out of tradition as it relates to sales. We take things too literally, and we try to race toward a sale instead of deepening a connection. Nothing deepens a connection more than *experiences* that you can do together. Some of my most impactful and fruitful sales meetings have been experiences: mountain biking at night, kiteboarding excursions, training for marathons, or helping someone write a book.

One of my favorite examples of a shared experience is my friends Marc Hodulich and Jesse Itzler's 29029 Everesting project where people climb the equivalent of Mt. Everest on a weekend at ski resorts in Idaho, Utah, and Vermont. Although the intention of these events is more personal endurance and pushing yourself, a byproduct is the incredible *new* powerful connections.

The 5 to 10 In-Person Touchpoints with Lots of Light Check-Ins

In all my interviews with some of the most successful leaders in the world as well as with some of the most sophisticated and accomplished sales professionals, I've heard the problem lies not in creating an initial touchpoint, but with *deepening* a relationship *and keeping it going.*

One way to achieve this effect is by shawshanking. It's a delicate dance of juggling frequency and check-ins with the prospect while also not getting annoying.

TL;DR

There has *never* been a world more ripe to create a connection economy all around yourself. Use tools and tactics to double down on your ability to create a more *genuine* connection. A byproduct of this will be the infinite possibilities it creates!

Make the Connection

- Find your greatest advocate and ask for just *one* referral from that person.
- Take the time that you spend on LinkedIn or other strategies that are lower on the hierarchy of connection and put it toward experiences or deepening relationships through shawshanking on social media.
- Come up with a creative event to bring your prospects together while adding value *without* selling.

CONCLUSION AND INVITATION

In February 2021, I was wrapping up a virtual retreat for 12 executives based on the ideas in this book. During this two-day period, I was able to see the transformation take place in a massively diverse crowd of male leaders. At the end of the retreat, I completely lost it. Not like a tear or two rolling down my cheek either, but full-on *heaving, slobbery* crying. To the executives in attendance, my losing it caught them by surprise. We had just completed a powerful event, so getting choked up would seem logical. But this was *way* beyond that.

As I tried to regain my composure, I looked around the Zoom screen and noticed a few awkward expressions on the screen. After a minute or two, I had finally regained enough composure to explain that the experience with them was the first time in my life that I was doing what it felt like I was put on this earth to do.

It's been my dream for as long as I can remember to make a positive impact on the world, to the point that I put impact above everything people typically want in their careers. Take this book, for example. Many authors write books with the goal of making money or building notoriety. That's not my goal. My goal is to make the results much more meaningful than that: my goal is to help everyone reading this book live a more fulfilling and prosperous life, whether they are making $40,000 or $4 million.

If you take nothing else from this book, take this: Life can be a ruthless pursuit of passion, and it requires tenacity and resilience. It's a never-ending process. You're always going to be graduating passions into currencies and then moving forward using your newest currency. That is the beauty of life and the power we have as individuals to make choices.

It's easy for people to look at me with my neon yellow glasses, tattoos everywhere, and a Rolodex full of people and say, "He's so extroverted that of course these things can work for him, but I'm *so* different."

But I'm just like you. Before I merged my passion with my purpose, I struggled a lot. It took hitting rock bottom in 2016 to help me see these things.

It also took me 64 interviews just to land a $28,000 a year entry-level job and four lateral moves.

But then I started doing the things I shared here.

I slowly became more and more "me," saving my asks …

And *that's* how I built my network to where it is today.

But this isn't just about me.

I've helped countless other people do the same.

From my friend Keoki who came from nothing in Hawaii and who has now just opened his own tattoo shop to my friend Bert Weiss with his podcast consultancy, or my friend Rob O'Kelly, who quit his job as a welder and who is now making three times more doing what he loves: building a car detailing empire.

And there's my good friend Stephen Churn, who mentioned the idea of creating Nerf gun parties for kids. I told him he can practice with my daughter's birthday party, and now he's created the ATL Dart Club. Remember the guy who wanted to punch me in the face? We are now best friends, and he's about to launch the largest project of his career in the next two months at Microsoft. It was all born from applying the strategies in this book.

The list goes on and on. This process has worked for countless people just like you.

So who will be the next person to save their asks and build a network, career, and personal life that fires them up, that creates an environment where work doesn't feel like *work*?! If you've made it this far, congratulations! You're *so* close to helping me achieve my goal of impacting one million lives.

And there's no reason that can't be you.

The worst thing you can do is nothing at all.

Just do something.

Do one thing.

Take one thing from this book and apply it to your life and watch the impact grow.

At this point, you probably feel like you know me, and I would like nothing more than for you to shawshank me. If you do, the most effective way is to connect with me on Instagram @tuff22 or on LinkedIn/christophertuff. Also check out my website for resources, information on retreats, and other materials at www.christuff.me.

If you want to shoot me an email (to the inbox where most emails go to die), you can reach me at chris@christuff.me.

Happy shawshanking!

ACKNOWLEDGMENTS

Thank you to everyone who made this book possible. A huge thank-you to my sister, Sarah Tuff, who helped me take this book from more than 40 interviews and put them into stories, and who told me at every turn that this book will help change the world. To my book and publishing consultant, Nick Pavlidis, who knows book structure, context, and strategy better than anyone else I know. Also, to the talented Ethan Webb and my copyeditor, Catherine Turner, who both helped make the content shine in this final form.

Thank you to my parents, who always made family a priority and who gave me all the opportunities to travel and learn. Also, to my mastermind, "The Great Eight," who cheered me on through the pandemic and helped teach me the essence of effective connection (Pete Boulden, Tommy Breedlove, Mike Domenicone, Taylor Barnes, Marc Hodulich, Hank McLarty, and Bert Weiss).

Thank you, Tyler Hartsook, who helps me fuel my addiction to momentum (and who tells me when to slow down) as well as Nicole Felicite, who always brings order to my chaos. To Keoki, who has inked some of my stories that I take with me everywhere I go and who helped with many of the Polynesian design elements in this book. To John Stapleton, who is the *best* designer in the world and helped with the book cover. Thank you, Nike and Brad

Kehm, for allowing me to test some of the content in the middle of a pandemic before it was fully ready. Also, to Justin Hegwood and Doug Stratton, who have allowed me to influence their own currencies and passions.

Thank you, Richard Ward and Erica Hoholick, who understand the power of words and connection, for allowing me to pursue my own passions.

And a *huge* thank-you to everyone who took the time to speak to me and whose stories and tactics make up most of this book. To Lydia Fenet, who took countless calls with me and who wrote such an incredible foreword. Quincy Jones, thank you for being a friend and for inspiring me to be a more effective networker and for renting those helicopters—as I say, no one can do what you do. Jasen Trautwein, I can't tell you how many people I've told about how you ruthlessly pursue your passions and "I love you, bruddah." Rory Cooper, if you've done it in D.C., you can do it anywhere! Vincent Pugliese, thanks for being a pioneer. Dan Miller, I'll never forget the seed you planted in me up at the sanctuary; you are the "OG." Alexander Gilkes, thanks for all you do and for walking the talk; I can't wait to see your companies take shape. Laurie Randall, I appreciate you and Nike for taking a vested interest in my project.

Astor Chambers, as a fellow father of girls and one of the most inspiring people I know, thanks for all your help and your amazing story. Ed Mathias, I'm so glad that I was able to hear how you helped build The Carlyle Group. Alexandra Wilkis Wilson, thanks for taking all the calls with me and for opening up some of your network to me (also on behalf of my daughters, I thank you for helping female entrepreneurs win). Craig Spodak, no one can connect the way you do, and the world is brighter with you in it (I'm also proud to call you a friend now). Candace Nelson, I'm so glad you were roommates with Sarah back at school; I can't wait to see what you bake up next. Robert Cohen, thanks for showing me how the sky's the limit and for taking the time to truly connect. Paul Brown, keep leading and "inspiring"; Atlanta and the restaurant industry are lucky to have you at the helm. Cary Franklin, thank you for helping me meet my wife, Julie, and for always showing me what connection looks like.

Dan Scalia, keep paving your own path and thanks for your authenticity and stories. Jeff Raider, my freshly shaved face and men worldwide thank you for your work and for setting the bar for what brand purpose looks like in application. Shelley Paxton, you are my true soul sister, and I thank you for the many hours you helped me hone my own purpose and understanding of impact. Karissa Kouchis, Tony Robbins is lucky to have you and thank you for always bringing "HAE" to every conversation. Randy Smith, you'll always be my favorite interview ever. Raimana Van Bastolaer, I love *you* and thanks for bringing light through surfing; I can't wait to hit Surf Ranch with you soon. Nathalie Molina Niño, thank you for challenging me and helping me see the world of passions in a new light.

Kerry Abner, you always inspire me and walk the talk, I'll always be your biggest advocate. Paul Ollinger, thank you for giving me some of the most important advice at the most opportune times. Dave Heath, I appreciate all your support and I will always wear your socks! Alex Molden, you are such an amazing role model for me as well as leaders across the U.S. I think you're just getting warmed up, baby.

Ken Hannaman, I can't wait to spend more time with you, and I believe in your path. Shane Emmett, I can't thank you enough for all the hours you've spent with me and for your genuine enthusiasm for books and my project. Bogdan Constantin, you're one of the best storytellers in the world—I can't wait to see how you inspire more. Justin Janowski, thanks for showing me how to be a bit more of an "askhole" and less of an "empty asker" and for pushing me out of my own comfort zones! Sean Reardon, I appreciate you meeting me in person during a pandemic; your stories will change lives. Farshid Arshid, thank you for the best sushi in the world and for first inspiring my initial comprehension of "currencies" and how to evolve them effectively. Geoff Clawson, who would have known that your time at Facebook would have impacted me so tremendously? The world is lucky to have your light. Aaron Abrahms, thanks for showing me how to network and sell and for introducing me to some of my favorite people; I can't wait to read *your* book. To Ryan O'Leary, Shane Needham, Derek White, Mitchell Crawford, and Jeff Baker, thank you for telling me to keep going after I shared some of the words in here with you.

A huge thanks to Jimmy Mills, who is always encouraging me to keep doing whatever it is I'm doing and for reading my drafts. A special shout-out to my brother Tommy Breedlove, to whom I attribute much of my path, and who pushed me to keep working on this manuscript when I thought I was done. To Tim Carroll, the biggest doubter in the room turned confidant and partner in crime, our Friday conversations made for more content, laughs, and a little bit of patience, and I can assure you these conversations fueled my soul just as much as they fueled yours (I can't wait for that sandy tennis ball).

And, last but not least, thank you to my publisher, Panta Press, and the incredible team of people working behind the scenes to help me share this important message with the world.

ABOUT THE AUTHOR

Chris is the national bestselling author of *The Millennial Whisperer*, which was released in February 2019 and quickly became a bestselling book at Barnes & Noble. His dynamic approach to attracting and motivating the next generation in the workplace has had him featured in *Forbes*, *Fast Company*, Fox TV, Cheddar News, and more.

Chris is also a partner at Guided by Good (22squared, Dendro, and Trade School), an advertising agency based out of Atlanta, where he practices all of the strategies in this book on a daily basis as the head of partnerships and growth.

Chris was one of the first marketers to work directly with Facebook in 2005 and became one of the foremost thought leaders in the digital space. He now also advises many start-ups in the Southeast, helping them with seed funding, new ideas, and connections.

When Chris isn't inspiring or connecting, he can be found with his two daughters, Finley and Marlin, and his wife, Julie, traveling, kiteboarding, and running.

You can connect with Chris on Instagram @tuff22 or at www.christuff.me.

A free ebook edition is available with the purchase of this book.

To claim your free ebook edition:

1. Visit MorganJamesBOGO.com
2. Sign your name CLEARLY in the space
3. Complete the form and submit a photo of the entire copyright page
4. You or your friend can download the ebook to your preferred device

A **FREE** ebook edition is available for you
or a friend with the purchase of this print book.

CLEARLY SIGN YOUR NAME ABOVE

Instructions to claim your free ebook edition:
1. Visit MorganJamesBOGO.com
2. Sign your name CLEARLY in the space above
3. Complete the form and submit a photo
   of this entire page
4. You or your friend can download the ebook
   to your preferred device

Print & Digital Together Forever.

Snap a photo

Free ebook

Read anywhere

CPSIA information can be obtained
at www.ICGtesting.com
Printed in the USA
JSHW020208030322
23536JS00002B/89

9 781631 956270